Local Organizations in Decentralized Development: Their Functions and Performance in India

Local Organizations in Decentralized Development: Their Functions and Performance in India

Ruth Alsop
Bryan Kurey

THE WORLD BANK
Washington, DC

ISBN-10: 0-8213-6312-3
ISBN-13: 978-0-8213-6312-6
e-ISBN: 0-8213-6313-1
DOI: 10.1596/978-0-8213-6312-6

Library of Congress Cataloging-in-Publication data has been applied for.

Cover photograph by: Declan McCullagh/mccullagh.org.
Cover design by: Serif Design Group.

Contents

Annex

Acknowledgments

This research was conducted as a collaborative venture between the World Bank's South Asia Environment and Social Development Unit, in Washington, DC; the Institute for Social and Economic Change (ISEC) in Bangalore, India; and international consultants from the Danish Centre for International Studies and Human Rights in Copenhagen and the Agricultural University of Norway in Oslo. Norwegian Trust Funds financed fieldwork and consultants.

The authors would first like to thank Dr. Rajasekhar and his team from the Institute for Social and Economic Change (ISEC) in Bangalore, India, for their unremitting and consistent partnership in an often-difficult and certainly time-consuming project. We would also like to recognize the inputs of the Samarthan team from Bhopal who worked with ISEC in data collection and entry. Other members of the research team deserving thanks are Dr. Olvar Bergland of the Agricultural University of Norway in Oslo for his superb econometric skills and his willingness to work through the night, and Dr. Neil Webster of the Danish Centre for International Studies and Human Rights in Copenhagen for his support during the development of survey instruments, early analysis, and drafting.

We are also in debt to those who provided comments on the research analysis and outputs. In particular, we are grateful to our peer reviewers for their valuable and constructive insights: Dr. Francois Vaillancourt of the University of Montreal; Dr. Ruth Mienzen-Dick of the International Food Policy Research Institute in Washington, DC; Dr. Dana Weist of the World Bank; and Dr. T. R. Raghunandan, Secretary for Rural Development and Panchayat Raj in the Government of Karnataka.

This research could not have been undertaken without funds from the Norwegian government or the support of managers in the South Asia Region of the World Bank.

List of Abbreviations

ARWSP	Advanced Rural Water Supply Program
CBO	Community-based organization
DFID	Department for International Development, United Kingdom
GAREMA	Gram Resources Management Association
GOI	Government of India
GOK	Government of Karnataka
GP	Gram panchayat
IRWES	Integrated Rural Water and Environment Sanitation Program
ISEC	Institute for Social and Economic Change
JFM	Joint forest management
JFMC	Joint Forest Management Committee
KAWAD	Karnataka Watershed Development Project
LD	Line department
LD-VL	Line department (village-level)
M&E	Monitoring and evaluation
NGO	Nongovernmental organization
NGO-VL	Nongovernmental organization (village-level)
PIA	Project implementation agency
PRI	Panchayat raj institution
SC	Scheduled caste
SGSY	Swarnajayanti Gram Swarozgar Yojna
SHG	Self-help group
TP	Taluk panchayat
WB	World Bank
ZP	Zilla panchayat

Glossary

Anganawadi	Village-based worker for women and child development programs
Gram panchayat	Village-level elected body
Gram sabha	Gathering of all villagers within the jurisdiction of a gram panchayat
Jal Sansthan	Corporation established by the Government of Uttar Pradesh, before State bifurcation, for the maintenance of water supply sources
Panchayat raj	Elected local government bodies
Stree-Shakthi	Government program for women's empowerment managed by the Department of Women and Child Development
Swajal	Term used as the name of a project and for the implementing NGO
Swa-Shakthi	World Bank- and IFAD-aided government program for Rural Women's Development and Empowerment (RWDEP), managed by a project office
Taluk panchayat	Block-level elected body
Van panchayat	Elected government unit in locations scheduled as tribal areas
Zilla panchayat	District-level elected body

I
Introduction

Local organizations are central actors in the rural development strategies sponsored by government and donor agencies in India.[1] Underlying their current prominence are, first, the 1992 constitutional amendments that paved the way for decentralization of government throughout India; second, concerns of efficiency and effectiveness that have led to increasing reliance on Indian nongovernmental organizations (NGOs) for local-level project implementation over the past two decades; and third, the rise in popularity of community-level membership organizations as mechanisms for local management of development resources and benefits.

However, many of these local organizations do not perform as expected, and development practitioners are uncertain about their effectiveness, fairness, and sustainability. Given the prevalence of local organizations and their high profile in contemporary development programs, these uncertainties need to be addressed. This document summarizes research that sought to meet this need. The study focused on local organizations involved in three sectors: rural women's development and empowerment; rural drinking water supply and sanitation; and watershed development. It sought to answer the following questions: (1) What types of organizations were working in each of the study sectors at the district level and below? (2) Which functions were these organizations mandated to perform? (3) What did they do in practice? (4) How well did organizations perform? (5) Which attributes—of an organization or of its context—contributed to better performance?

The study used a mixed methodology, drawing on both secondary sources and primary information. Using a range of instruments and techniques, fieldworkers collected data from representatives and staff of organizations implementing programs at different administrative levels in the three sectors, from villagers and elected bodies in the study sites, and from households receiving sector benefits. Organizational and functional typologies were central to the analysis. The first comprised 26 types of organizations falling into four broad categories: government organizations (elected and administrative); project organizations; private organizations (for profit and not-for-profit); and community-based organizations (CBOs). These operated at different levels—national, district, subdistrict (block), and village. The functional typology included nine broad functions: financing,

1

staffing, provisioning, community-based action, capacity building, coordination of activities, monitoring and evaluation (M&E), conflict resolution/accountability, and information sharing/dissemination. Each broad function was subdivided to give 39 subfunctions. Analytic techniques ranged from analysis of narrative reports through descriptive statistics to econometrics.

The research was undertaken in the states of Karnataka, Madhya Pradesh, and Uttaranchal. For each study sector, data were gathered from a total of four districts in two states. The number of villages covered was 71 in the women's development sector, 72 in the drinking water and sanitation sector, and 69 in the watershed sector. A total of 345 village-level CBOs, 49 project organizations, 204 panchayat raj institutions (PRIs), and 151 line agencies were investigated. In all, interviews were held with 3,311 individual members of village-level organizations. In each study village, an organizational inventory was undertaken, poverty and performance rankings were done, transect walks were used to build a village profile, focus groups were conducted with members of local organizations, and in-depth case studies were undertaken. The Indian research organization collaborating in the study also held district- and state-level meetings to verify findings, draw out explanations, and ascertain what the implications of the findings might be for the design and implementation of decentralized interventions.

The conceptual framework guiding the research was based on the premise that an organization's assets, processes, linkages, and context determine its performance. Performance of a range of organizational functions and achievement of development outcomes were assessed based on three criteria: effectiveness, equity, and sustainability. Assessment of assets examined data on the human, material, and financial assets of organizations. Assessment of processes involved examining an organization's internal transparency and accountability. Linkages analyzed were those with other organizations. Finally, context analysis involved examining the physiographic, social, and infrastructure characteristics of the location in which an organization operated.

As rural development approaches in India increasingly stress decentralized resource management and control, two debates dominate discourse on the roles of local organizations in this process. The first is a practical one on how to make local organizations perform effectively. The second focuses on the relative functions of government organizations—both elected local governments and administrative line departments (LDs)—and different forms of NGOs, including the private sector and community groups at the local level. The empirical research reported here suggests that the debates on effectiveness and relative functions cannot be separated. At present, interventions struggle with suboptimal performance of local organizations, indicating that different configurations of a plural organizational landscape, in which local government organizations are an integral part, are required for the effective delivery and sustainability of different development benefits.

Research findings indicate that local administrative government bodies (LDs) are deeply involved, and largely effective, in the execution of projects. Elected local governments (gram, tuluk, and zilla panchayats), however, currently have only limited roles and are often ineffective in performing their assigned functions. Community-level membership organizations function as extensions of project implementation structures, performing functions associated with the distribution of short-term project benefits. The sustainability of these organizations and that of the benefits they deal with is highly questionable and while multistakeholder coordination committees exist, in practice they meet rarely, comprise a limited range of stakeholders, focus mainly on administrative monitoring, and provide little in the way of strategic guidance for interventions. The presence of NGOs working independently of external interventions is low—with most acting as contractors for government programs—and the private sector is virtually inoperative in the sectors studied.

Local organizations, of whatever provenance, clearly require—but are often not receiving or generating on their own—sufficient financial assets to perform the roles expected of them. Furthermore, while less important than the influence of finance on quality of performance, other organizational attributes, including human and material assets and internal organizational processes, carry varying but significant degrees of importance depending on the type of benefit being delivered. In part because of this complexity, achieving the optimal "mix" in project design of both up-front investments in assets and distribution of functions has proven difficult, resulting in mixed outcomes in terms of the equity and sustainability of organizations and project benefits.

While the research outlined in this paper took place in India, experience suggests that the findings may be appropriate to other countries where rural development depends on the effective performance of decentralized organizations both for implementation and as the medium for local-level empowerment.[2]

The remainder of this section briefly outlines current thinking on the importance of local organizations in decentralized interventions and then describes the conceptual framework and methodology used in this research. Section II moves into a description of findings, beginning with mandated functions of the different types of organizations and then on to an analysis of how those functions are performed. Sections III through V examine the factors associated with different levels of performance: assets, processes, linkages, and context. Section VI then assesses the equity and sustainability aspects of performance. Finally, section VII draws together the main findings and summarizes operational implications.

Background: Local Organizations and Decentralization

While decentralization of government has been attempted periodically within states in postindependent India, the central government first articulated it as a national priority in the 73rd and 74th constitutional amendments in 1992. Decentralization takes a variety of forms, not all of which promote greater citizen participation or seek to devolve decision making to lower level authorities. Where decentralization reforms pursue a strategy of devolution, they involve the transfer of significant political, administrative, and fiscal responsibilities to local elected bodies and/or administrative (LD) governments. Such reforms are premised on the belief that localization improves linkages to local communities, which is intended to enhance transparency and accountability of development activities, governance, and service delivery. It is also intended to enable communities to become involved in collective decision making over local resource allocation and management. The ultimate objective is the empowerment of citizens in their relations with the state.

In practice, however, decentralization reforms have enjoyed mixed success. The problems are many and complex, but factors commonly influencing less-than-desired outcomes include the following: unwillingness on the part of central, state, and substate governments to devolve significant powers or resources to implement the activities provided for by legislation; the paucity of funds—particularly untied funds—available to transfer to local bodies, and the lack of a revenue base at the local level; the problem of local elites capturing decentralized organizations and the accompanying resources; the inability of local government organizations to respond to local needs and priorities; the lack of accountability of service providers to citizens; and the poor design of decentralized interventions by governments and donor agencies.[3]

To address some of these issues, central governments and development organizations are placing greater responsibility on local organizations. Local organizations are by their nature closer to citizens, and thus, it is argued, more capable of understanding and responding to them. Among other functions, these organizations are considered to be useful in the following:

- Determining resource or staffing needs at the local level;
- Engaging citizens, their elected representatives, and government staff (LD) in planning actions and budget expenditures;
- Raising resources and implementing community-level projects, such as road-building or school maintenance;
- Ensuring local monitoring of expenditures, processes, and outcomes;
- Improving accountability of the state and elected representatives to citizens;

- Resolving local-level conflicts; and
- Disseminating information in locally appropriate ways.

Conceptual Framework

Despite their growing popularity, many of these local organizations do not perform as expected, and development practitioners are uncertain about their effectiveness, fairness, and sustainability. This document seeks to shed light on what factors influence the quality of an organization's performance. It presents data from research focused on local organizations involved in three sectors in the states of Karnataka, Madhya Pradesh, and Uttaranchal: rural women's development and empowerment; rural drinking water supply and sanitation; and watershed development (annex table A3). The research sought to answer the following questions: (1) What types of organizations were working in each of the study sectors at the district level and below? (2) Which functions were these organizations mandated to perform? (3) What did they do in practice? (4) How well did organizations perform? (5) Which attributes contributed to better performance?

Typologies of the variety of organizations at the local level and the range of functions that those organizations perform were key in the analysis of organizational performance.

Organizational Typology

Following North (1990), this paper defines *organizations* as "groups of individuals, bound by a common purpose, involving a defined set of authority relations and dedicated to achieving objectives." Organizations differ from *institutions,* which are defined as rules of the game and include "codes of conduct, norms of behavior and conventions" (North 1990; Uphoff 1986). Institutions are both embedded in and surround organizations.

Local organizations, defined in this study as those operating at the district level and below, are divided into four general analytic categories (box 1): government organizations, project organizations, private organizations, and CBOs.

This organizational typology allows categorization of local organizations at any given administrative level—the state, district, subdistrict, and village. Annex table A1 provides summary figures on which types of organization were found in each location studied.

Functions of Local Organizations

A typology of nine major functions was developed, and data were collected on 39 subfunctions within these nine categories (annex table A2). The major

---

Box 1 Main Categories of the Organizational Typology

Government organizations

- *Administrative government organizations:* These include all organizational entities staffed by government employees, general civil servants (secretaries and other Indian Administrative Service/state cadre officers) and line department staff.
- *Elected government organizations:* National and state level politicians were not included in the sample. The sample included zilla panchayats (ZP) at the district level; taluk panchayats (TP), also called panchayat samitis, at the block level; and gram panchayats (GP) at the village level.

Project organizations
These are created by the sector programs or projects in order to oversee implementation activities at the district, block, or village level. At the district and block levels, these project organizations fall into two categories: those especially created as new agencies to manage specific interventions; and existing nongovernmental organizations (NGOs) co-opted by projects.

Private organizations
These include organizations that are managed independently in each of the sectors studied. Organizations of this type include *private for-profit organizations* (of which this study covers very few) and *private nonprofit organizations* (mostly those recognized as NGOs).

Community-based organizations (CBOs)
CBOs are membership organizations based on collective action and are found almost entirely at the village level. They can be categorized into four types: self-initiated, self-evolved CBOs; NGO-initiated CBOs; government-initiated CBOs; and project-initiated CBOs, which are initiated as part of an intervention.

---

functions include the following:

- *Financing* involves mobilizing and securing funds and other resources that support the work of local organizations.
- *Staffing* covers the provision of staff by an organization to form or support groups elsewhere.
- *Provisioning* is defined as activities that facilitate access to services, resources, and local assets. The specific form of provisioning depends on the project's subsector.
- *Community-based action* covers physical construction and mobilization of village resources by group members.

- *Capacity building* covers facilitation or direct provision of training programs.
- *Coordination of activities* refers to coordination with other organizations of the same type or of different types and at different levels (village, block, and district).
- *Monitoring and evaluation (M&E)* refers to activities undertaken to track organizational inputs, outputs, and performance.
- *Conflict resolution and accountability* covers activities that can prevent conflict, such as regular meetings between different local organizations, as well as direct activities to resolve disputes, such as mediation and adjudication.
- *Information sharing and dissemination* involves sharing information within and among local organizations.

Measuring Performance of Local Organizations

Analysis of performance tells us what different organizations do and how well they do it. Studies undertaken in recent years demonstrate that four factors play significant roles in shaping an organization's performance: assets, processes, linkages, and context.[4] The first three of these are attributes particular to an organization, while the last relates to the environment in which the organization and its members operate. This is schematically presented in figure 1.

Three dimensions of performance are explored in this paper: effectiveness, equity, and sustainability. Effectiveness is measured through an assessment of the quality of performance of functions and delivery of development outcomes; equity is measured by looking at participation in an organization's activities and the distribution of development benefits; and

Figure 1 Schematic Representation of the Conceptual Framework

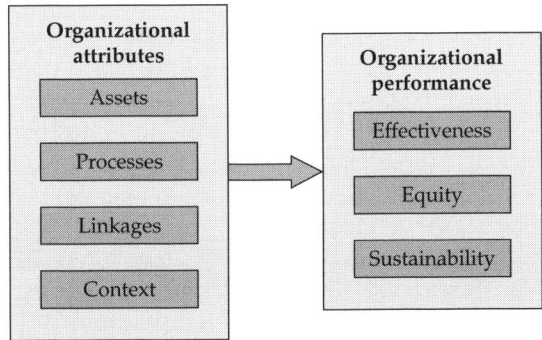

Source: Authors' creation.

sustainability is measured on the basis of organizational independence and continuation of benefit streams.

The four factors hypothesized as causal in organizational performance are measured using clusters of variables as indicators of the following:[5]

- Assets. Human, material, and financial assets are considered. Human assets include the quantity and quality of human resources, while material assets include physical resources. Financial assets refer to the monetary resources of an organization.
- Processes. Three key process variables are measured: knowledge of organizational rules, transparency of operation, and decision-making processes.
- Linkages. Variables include the number and form of linkages with line agencies, PRIs, and other organizations working in a study sector.
- Context. These variables include the physiographic, social, infrastructural, and state context of the location in which an organization operates.

Methodology

The study used a mixed methodology comprising: (a) extensive data collection based on standard instruments, including semistructured interviews and seven different questionnaires (annex table A4); and (b) an intensive inquiry using interactive techniques (focus groups, case studies, and a range of participatory rural appraisal tools) to obtain more nuanced information on variables, including social context, quality of organizational participation, equity in processes, and quality of collective action.[6]

In each of the three states (Karnataka, Madhya Pradesh, and Uttaranchal), two districts for each sector were sampled. Selection criteria included indices of modernization of agriculture, dependence on agricultural/other primary production sectors and human resource development, and presence of a sector development intervention.[7] From each district, three blocks were randomly selected from a list of those in which there were program or project interventions. Within each block six villages with interventions were randomly selected.[8] In each village, stratified random sampling, based on a poverty ranking exercise, was used to select eight households with membership in the organizations financed by the World Bank–aided project (or in the case of Karnataka watersheds, a project financed by the UK Department for International Development [DFID]), and eight that were members of other local organizations operating in the same sector.[9]

On the basis of this sampling framework, data collection covered 212 villages, 3,311 households, 345 village-level CBOs, 49 project organizations, 204 PRIs (elected government bodies), and 151 line agencies (administrative government) across all three sectors. These are categorized by type of local organization and sector in annex table A5.

Notes

1. Local organizations are defined for this study as all types of organizations working at the district level and below.

2. Empowerment is defined as the process of enhancing an individual's or group's capacity to make choices and to translate those choices into effective outcomes (Alsop and Heinsohn 2005).

3. See Bahl 2002; Bardhan and Mookherjee 1999; Bird 2002; Dreze and Sen 1996; Hirway 1989; Jodha 1992; Manor 1995; Ostrom, Schroeder, and Wynne 1993; Parker 1995; Prud'homme 1995; Tanzi 1995; Walker 1991; Westergaard and Alam 1995; World Bank 2000.

4. See, for example, Ahmed 1999; Buckley 1996; Ghatak and Guinnane 1999; Kolavalli and Kerr 2002; Morduch 1999; Narayan 1995; Rajakutty 1997; Sharma and Zeller 1997; Uphoff 1997; Uphoff, Esman, and Krishna 1998; Wenner 1995; White and Runge 1995.

5. The direct impact of assets, processes, linkages, and context on organizational performance can be statistically established only in the case of effectiveness of an organization's performance of functions. While it is possible that these factors also impact organizational performance in terms of equity and sustainability, the data collected here do not allow for such links to be conclusively established. The data do enable, however, an analysis of equity and sustainability as indicators of the quality of organizational performance, as detailed in section VI.

6. Information derived using interactive and semistructured approaches provided insight about how to specify and interpret quantitatively identified associations. They also allowed exploration of specific issues and the preparation of case studies. In addition to primary data collection, the Indian research collaborator also held state- and district-level workshops. These workshops considered draft sector findings, allowing for verification, enhanced interpretation, and discussion of implications.

7. A detailed research protocol is available from the author on request.

8. Of these six villages, five had projects supported by the World Bank—or the UK's Department for International Development (DFID) in the case of Karnataka watersheds—in a given sector. One had a project not supported by the World Bank in the same sector. For the purposes of this study, we conflate World Bank–aided and DFID-aided projects. All references to local organizations induced by World Bank–aided projects also cover those induced by DFID-aided projects.

9. In practice, the sample was slightly smaller than anticipated and distributed differently in the watershed sector. The former occurred because in some villages there were limited numbers of community-based organization (CBOs), and in other cases some CBOs had few members. The latter occurred because the Karnataka Watershed Development Project (KAWAD) operated only in three districts and in three blocks of those districts.

II
Performance of Mandated Functions

Mandated functions are defined as those found assigned in project documentation, legislation, or similar secondary sources. This section begins by describing the functions mandated, by design, to organizations at different administrative levels and begins to illustrate planned patterns of comparative advantage for different organizations in decentralized settings. Following this, the frequency with which organizations actually perform these mandated functions is reviewed. This allows for analysis of both the extent to which project designers effectively allocate functions, as well as the ways in which local organizations take on such assignments and adapt to conditions on the ground. Finally, the section assesses quality of performance of functions by organization.

Mandated Functions of Organizations

Table 1 outlines mandated functions for organizations at different levels in each sector and highlights a number of points. First, the work of *state-level organizations* (both government and nongovernment) is wide-ranging, but it is directed primarily at facilitating or undertaking the macrolevel functions necessary for strategic management (staffing and coordination), financing, M&E, and maintaining information systems. This is true across all three sectors studied. These functions are less likely to be assigned to organizations below the state level (particularly staffing and coordination), indicating that state-level administrative government bodies and project organizations are viewed as having a particular comparative advantage in these areas.

At the *district level*, elected government bodies are mandated responsibility for financing, community-based action, M&E, and conflict resolution (except in women's development). District-level administrative governments are frequently mandated functions in these same areas, with the exception of conflict resolution. Project organizations are also mandated to carry out similar functions, with the added responsibilities of capacity building (except in the case of women's development), coordination, conflict resolution (except in the watershed development sector), and information dissemination. At the *block level*, project organizations are mandated a wide range of functions. Administrative government bodies are also mandated to perform several functions at the block level, but only in the women's development and watershed development sectors.

Table 1 also shows that elected governments have a greater level of mandated responsibilities at the *village level* than at any other level, and are more often mandated responsibilities than any other organization at the village level. Gram panchayats (GPs) have responsibility for M&E and conflict resolution in all three sectors, and are given several additional functions in the water supply and sanitation sector. Also of note is that the village level is the only place where NGOs are mandated functions, in this case banks (in the women's development sector) and CBOs.[10] Project organizations have widespread responsibilities at the village level in the watershed development sector, but they are mandated no responsibilities in the other two sectors.

In sum, project designers spread mandated functions widely across sectors, among government and project organizations, and at various administrative levels. Project organizations are mandated functions at all administrative levels, although their role is quite limited at the village level, where only the watershed development sector assigns responsibilities. Elected government bodies, while holding considerable responsibilities at the village level, are mandated no functions at the state or block levels. Administrative government bodies at the block and village levels have only limited responsibilities. In addition,

- In rural water supply and sanitation projects, functions are mandated to administrative government at all levels in the areas of resource allocation (financing, staffing, provisioning).
- In the women's development sector this is reversed, with functions mandated to administrative government at all levels in the areas of capacity building and information.
- In the watershed development sector, by contrast, these organizations have no mandated responsibilities below the state level.

Finally, there appears to be considerable duplication of mandated functions in all sectors, particularly at the state and district levels, as well as at the block and village levels in the watershed development sector. This may not be a problem if the project's design and implementation are good and if functions are undertaken in a coordinated manner. However, as evidence presented later demonstrates, this is rarely the case.

Actual Functions Performed by Local Organizations

Analysis of functions actually undertaken indicates that the frequency with which they are performed is significantly lower than envisaged in project design. In addition, many organizations undertake functions for which they

Table 1 Mandated Functions of Organizations: Women's Development and Empowerment Sector (W), Drinking Water Supply and Sanitation Sector (D), and Watershed Development Sector (H)

Local organization type	Financing	Staffing	Provisioning	Community-based action	Capacity building	Coordination	M&E	Conflict resolution	Information
State level									
Administrative government	W D	W D H		W D H	W	W D H	W D H		W H
Project organizations	W D H	W D H		W D H	W H	W D H	W D H	D H	D H
District level									
Administrative government	W D		D	W D	W	W	W D		W
Elected government (zilla panchayat)	D H	D		W D H			W D H	D H	
Project organizations	H	D	H	W D H	D H	W D H	W D H	W D	W D H

12

Block level																	
Administrative government	D			W D		W D		W		W		W		W			
Project organizations		H	W D H	D H	W	W D H		H W	D H	H W		W D H		H	W	D H	
Village level																	
Administrative government	D		D		D		W		W		W				W		
Elected government (gram panchayat)	D		D		D						W D		W D H		W	D H	
Banks[a]	W			W		W		W		W		W					
Project organizations		H	H		H		H		H		H		H		H		H
Community-based organizations	W D		D		W D H		D		D		W D H		W D H		W	D H	W D

Sources: GOI 1999, 2002a, 2002b; GOK 2001, 2002; KAWAD 1995, 2002; World Bank 1993, 1997, 2001.

Note: This table summarizes information for sectors; therefore, while information for each sector relates to a series of interventions, differences among different types of intervention are not noted. M&E = monitoring and evaluation.

a. Banks are difficult to classify as they are run on quasi-commercial lines and operate outside of a line agency structure, but they have a major vested interest by government.

have no mandate. Three general tendencies emerge from the research and are discussed in detail below:

• Functions mandated to support organizations are often undertaken by local organizations that they have initiated, indicating **subsidiarity;**
• Mandated functions are often **transferred** among local organizations; and
• **Elected governments** (panchayats) consistently fail to undertake mandated functions.

Subsidiarity and Transference

While subsidiarity is practiced in all three sectors studied, the watershed development sector illustrates the pattern well. The actual functions undertaken by village-level organizations in this sector are presented in table 2. This table also indicates whether each function is (a) mandated to the support organization that initiated the local organization but not to the local organization itself; (b) mandated to the local organization itself; or (c) not mandated to either the local organization or its initiating support organization. The first tells us whether subsidiarity is occurring, that is, whether an organization is taking on functions allocated to a higher-level body. The second tells us whether an organization is undertaking the tasks it is mandated. The third tells us whether, in practice, organizations are operating without mandate.

Over three-quarters of government-initiated CBOs in the watershed sector and 61 percent of project-initiated CBOs undertake financing activities, even though this task is mandated only for their support organization. Similarly, the NGO-initiated CBO operating in this sector undertakes financing, provisioning, capacity building, M&E, and conflict resolution functions mandated to its support organizations. Almost all (92 percent) of the 59 project-initiated CBOs studied in this sector undertake capacity building, a function mandated to their support organization.

The women's development and empowerment sector reinforces this (for conflict resolution and information), and also illustrates the prevalence of transferring functions among local organizations. This is indicated by organizations not performing functions mandated to them (those with a letter b in table 3) when others—without a mandate—perform that same function (those with a letter c in table 3). Table 3 indicates transferring staffing, coordination, M&E, and conflict resolution functions. In terms of coordination, for example, only 32 percent of organizations mandated to carry out this function (government-initiated CBOs) actually undertake it. By contrast, while coordination is not mandated to the village-level NGO (NGO-VL)

Table 2 Functions Undertaken by Village-Level Local Organizations, Watershed Development Sector

(Percentage of local organizations of each type)

Local organization type	N	Financing	Staffing	Provisioning	Community-based action	Capacity building	Coordination	M&E	Conflict resolution	Information
Elected government	43	13[a]	12[c]	24[c]	0[a]	6[c]	17[c]	27[b]	5[b]	33[a]
Government-initiated CBO	9	78[a]	22[c]	89[b]	33[b]	100[c]	44[c]	67[b]	78[b]	56[c]
NGO-initiated CBO	1	100[a]	0[c]	100[a]	0[a]	100[a]	100[c]	100[a]	100[a]	0[c]
Project-initiated CBO	59	61[a]	14[b]	95[b]	41[b]	92[a]	66[b]	85[b]	71[b]	86[b]

Source: Local organization officials questionnaire, watershed development sector.

Note: CBO = community-based organization; M&E = monitoring and evaluation.

a. The local organization does not have a mandate to undertake activities in this function area, but the support organization does.

b. Mandated function for the local organization.

c. Not mandated to the local organization or to its initiating support organization.

Table 3 Functions Undertaken by Village-Level Local Organizations, Women's Development and Empowerment Sector

(Percentage of local organizations of each type)

Local organization type	N	Financing	Staffing	Provisioning	Community-based action	Capacity building	Coordination	M&E	Conflict resolution	Information
Line department	n.a.	n.a.	n.a.	n.a.	n.a.	0[b]	n.a.	n.a.	0[b]	0[b]
GP/GS	n.a.	n.a.	n.a.	n.a.	n.a.	n.a.	n.a.	0[b]	0[b]	n.a.
NGO (village)	1	0[c]	0[c]	0[c]	0[c]	100[a]	100[c]	0[a]	0[a]	0
Government-initiated CBO	56	50[b]	11[c]	78[b]	18[b]	77[c]	32[b]	59[c]	77[c]	50[b]
NGO-initiated CBO	11	45[b]	9[b]	100[b]	9[b]	55[c]	64[c]	36[c]	55[c]	36[a]
Project-initiated CBO	60	55[b]	30[c]	93[b]	35[b]	90[c]	70[c]	80[b]	82[b]	68[b]
Self-initiated CBO	2	50[b]	0[c]	50[b]	50[b]	100[c]	50[c]	50[c]	100[a]	50[a]

Source: Local organization officials questionnaire, women's development and empowerment sector.

Note: GP = gram panchayat; GS = gram sabha; M&E = monitoring and evaluation.

n.a. Not applicable.

a. The local organization does not have a mandate to undertake activities in this function area, but the support organization that initiated it does.

b. Mandated function for the local organization.

c. Not mandated to the local organization or to its initiating support organization.

16

operating in this sector, it does perform this function, as do 70 percent of project-initiated CBOs, and one of the two self-initiated CBOs.

Transferring coordination, M&E, and conflict resolution functions is also commonly found in the drinking water supply and sanitation sector (annex table A6).

In sum, while functions are being undertaken, in none of the three sectors is there a close correlation between functions mandated and functions undertaken. In nearly half (48 percent) of all cases, functions mandated to a specific type of organization are not performed. It is to be expected that, as a project or program is implemented, the functional requirements of organizations may change from the original vision. Poor project design, changes in contexts, the subsequent implementation of other projects in the same localities, and changes in the situations and conditions of beneficiaries can all have significant consequences for operational functions. A mandate to perform a function is therefore not a guarantee that a local organization will actually undertake the function, and many functions are undertaken that are not mandated.

Performance of Decentralized Local Government Organizations

Legislation on local government enacted as part of India's overall decentralization program gives a broad set of responsibilities to village-level elected governments (that is, GPs) in all three states covered by the study. These include conflict resolution and minor law and order issues. GPs are also accorded a degree of responsibility with respect to development activities, including making needs assessments and implementing a number of programs such as employment assurance schemes, pension schemes, housing programs for the poor, and relief work.

In line with these responsibilities, the expectation is that GPs would undertake such functions as coordination of activities, conflict resolution, and M&E. However, despite these formally assigned roles, this research found that GPs did not generally undertake such activities in the sectors studied. Only when a GP is directly involved in a specific project's implementation are these functions performed. Box 2 illustrates how problems can arise when GPs do not show an active interest in performing the functions expected of them.

The watershed development sector provides an illustration of the low frequency in undertaking functions by local elected government. In this sector, GPs have mandates with respect to project M&E and conflict resolution. However, household survey responses indicate that these functions were rarely undertaken. As table 4 shows, only 3.5 percent of households in Karnataka, and 3.7 percent of households in Uttaranchal noted that GPs performed conflict resolution activities. In Karnataka, M&E was performed even less frequently than conflict resolution (1.8 percent). In Uttaranchal,

Table 4 Functions Undertaken by Gram Panchayats, Watershed Development Sector

| | Percentage responses from households under differently managed interventions | | | |
| | Karnataka | | Uttaranchal | |
Function (*Mandated functions noted in bold*)	*KAWAD* (N = 455)	*Line department and JFMC* (N = 112)	*GAREMA* (N = 430)	*Line department and JFM/Van panchayat* (N = 124)
Resolving conflicts within the local organization	**3.5**	**0.0**	**3.7**	**14.5**
Mobilizing benefits from the government (funds and so on) and banks	5.3	3.6	20.9	21.0
Providing financial assistance (pension to widows, agricultural laborers, support toward housing, loans, and so on) to vulnerable groups	24.2	16.1	81.4	99.2
Sending GP staff to help local organizations perform functions	0.4	0.0	19.1	33.9
Instructing line department staff to provide technical support (such as extension services) to members	2.4	6.3	22.6	25.8
Providing the GP building for local organization meetings	0.4	0.9	12.3	10.5
Providing village tanks, grazing lands, trees, and so on for collective income-generating activities	9.9	9.8	9.3	32.3
Providing income-generating opportunities	0.4	3.6	18.8	21.0

Providing community assets (roads, child care centers, and so on)	27.7	22.3	17.2	63.7
Facilitating training from agriculture, horticulture departments	0.7	0.0	18.1	6.5
Coordinating with line departments to ensure that benefits (seeds, saplings, and so on) reach members	1.3	2.7	25.1	37.1
Coordinating with other local organizations for resource convergence	0.9	0.9	17.7	12.9
Monitoring local organization activities	**0.0**	**1.8**	**40.2**	**66.9**
Ensuring that the local organization is accountable to members	0.2	0.0	27.4	16.9
Ensuring that the local organization incorporates the interests of the poor and vulnerable	5.7	4.5	36.5	19.4
Sharing information on GP programs with local organization members	9.7	0.0	59.8	62.9

Source: Household questionnaire.

Note: GAREMA = Gram Resources Management Association; GP = gram panchayat; JFM = joint forest management; JFMC = Joint Forest Management Committee; KAWAD = Karnataka Watershed Development Project.

Box 2 Difficulties Working with Gram Panchayats

The Swa-Shakthi women's group in Jangamanahalli prepared proposals to obtain benefits such as a community hall and loans under SGSY from the gram panchayat. Despite their efforts, nothing generated a positive response. According to the president, who was also a ward member in the gram panchayat (GP), no one even bothered to tell the women's group the status of their proposals. Similarly, the Swa-Shakthi group in Nakkanahalli in Kolar district requested the GP to provide a site for construction of a meeting hall, or allow the group to conduct its meetings in the GP office. The GP did neither. As a result, the meetings had to be conducted in a temple, where a few of the members' belongings were stolen.

In Maradaghatta village in Kolar district, the Swa-Shakthi group obtained training from their support organization on how to obtain benefits from GPs. The group, consisting of scheduled caste (SC) households, was apprehensive that the sharp caste divisions that had emerged in the village between the dominant Reddys and the lower-status SCs would keep them from obtaining benefits. The support organization staff took the group leaders and a few members to the GP to petition for allocation of a site to construct a meeting hall. The GP allotted the group a building site located in a supposedly vacant space between the main village, where the Reddys reside, and the SC colony. However, this became a problem when it was found that the lot had already been encroached by a Reddy household.

At the same time, the location of the allotted building site became a source of conflict. The Reddys in the community argued that the meeting hall should be built in the main village for the benefit of everyone, while the SC households maintained that it should be built in the SC colony as the request had been made by a group from the colony. This secondary conflict over where the hall should be built overshadowed the most immediate issue—that a common property had been encroached. Rather than enforce its original decision regarding the location of the meeting hall and take up the issue of removing the encroachers from the land, the GP stated that the larger conflict over its location should be resolved first.

Source: Case studies.

---

however, while still low, around half of all GPs undertook M&E. The vast majority of GPs in Uttaranchal also played a key financing role and, while still averaging low involvement, did tend to be more involved across functions than their counterparts in Karnataka.

The case is similar in the women's development sector (annex table A7), in which responses to the household survey indicated that village-level elected governments rarely undertook any functions, mandated or otherwise. This was corroborated by presidents of GPs working in the study locations, who said they had nothing to do with women's development and empowerment and that they undertook functions related to providing financial assistance to "vulnerable groups" (presumably including women), implementing construction works, and maintaining basic infrastructure.

In the water supply and sanitation sector, by contrast, GPs are reported to much more consistently undertake mandated (and to some extent nonmandated functions) than in the other sectors (annex table A8). When they are charged with a substantial role in coordinating the water supply scheme, as in the Advanced Rural Water Supply Program (ARWSP) and to a lesser extent the Integrated Rural Water and Environment Sanitation Program (IRWES)—both in Karnataka—GPs perform mandated and many nonmandated functions, including those associated with delivery of benefits.[11] However, in schemes in which LDs, NGOs (Swajal), or local corporations (Jal Sansthan) are given primary responsibility for managing the scheme, performance of functions in this sector are reduced considerably. GPs perform best across programs in this sector in sending staff to local organizations and providing facilities for meetings. In these, as in most other functions, elected governments in Karnataka undertake functions far more frequently than those in Uttaranchal.

Quality of Organizational Performance

Functions undertaken are not necessarily functions performed well. Broadly, as table 5 indicates, village-level organizations are rated as good or, more often, adequate in performance of functions. However, that responses are concentrated in the "adequate" category indicates that there is room for improvement.

Examination of these figures indicates that, while performance of functions across sectors appears to be generally good in organizational administration and management (financing, M&E, and conflict resolution), ratings are weighted toward "adequate" on quality of performance in more development-oriented functions, notably community-based action (55.7 percent adequate and 23.5 percent poor, versus 20.8 percent good) and coordination (48.5 percent adequate versus 31.3 percent good).[12]

Further investigation of this pattern—using household survey responses on quality of performance of a variety of functions by local support organizations and village-level elected governments—confirms this observation. Local support organizations in the women's development sector were

Table 5 Quality of Performance of Functions by Village-Level Organizations

| | Performance | | | |
Function	Poor (%)	Adequate (%)	Good (%)	N^a
Financing	15.4	39.2	45.4	230
Staffing	21.2	48.6	30.2	102
Provisioning	24.0	43.1	32.9	320
Community-based action	23.5	55.7	20.8	213
Capacity building	14.0	41.3	44.7	317
Coordination of activity	20.2	48.5	31.3	269
Monitoring and evaluation	8.8	38.7	52.5	293
Conflict resolution/accountability	15.7	36.1	48.2	299
Information sharing/dissemination	17.2	47.3	35.5	280
Average	17.8	44.3	37.9	

Source: Household questionnaire.
a. Number of local organizations undertaking these functions across all sectors and including all organizational types.

found to perform basic functions such as formation of groups, provision of savings and credit services, conflict resolution, and monitoring quite well. But broader development and empowerment functions, especially those not related to savings and credit, were poorly done. Table 6 provides feedback from households on performance of support organizations in projects within this sector. In Karnataka, management and administration functions received a good rating on average, with the responses ranging from a low of 66 percent in providing capable staff, to nearly 94 percent for local organization formation. Support organizations in Madhya Pradesh received similarly favorable ratings for these functions.

In both states, good ratings for performance of development-oriented functions by support organizations were much less frequent. In Karnataka, good ratings ranged from an average of 41 percent for training in income generation activities, to a high of almost 70 percent for coordination with other local organizations. Numbers are perhaps slightly higher in Madhya Pradesh, but good ratings still do not exceed 70 percent, on average, for development functions.

Much like the women's empowerment sector, the tendency among support organizations in both the drinking water supply and sanitation sector and the watershed development sectors was to undertake basic administrative functions well, but not development functions (annex tables A9 and A10).

Table 6 Performance of Functions by Support Organizations, Women's Development and Empowerment Sector

Percentage responses from households under differently managed interventions citing good performance

Function	Karnataka				Madhya Pradesh			
	Swa-Shakthi *(N = 257)*	*Stree-Shakthi* *(N = 220)*	*Others* *(N = 75)*	*Average*	*Swa-Shakthi* *(N = 290)*	*SGSY* *(N = 155)*	*Others* *(N = 58)*	*Average*
Administration and Management								
Formation of the local organization	98.4	88.6	94.7	93.9	88.6	86.5	93.1	89.4
Explaining how to manage the group	96.1	75.5	81.3	84.3	88.3	70.3	93.1	83.9
Providing books for accounts maintenance	92.6	70.0	74.7	79.1	85.5	74.8	89.7	83.3
Monitoring the local organization activities	91.4	69.5	72.0	77.6	80.7	61.9	89.7	77.4
Resolving conflicts within the group	90.7	71.8	62.7	75	83.4	65.8	91.4	80.2
Ensuring that the local organization is accountable to members	75.1	67.7	62.7	68.5	85.2	57.4	89.7	77.4
Providing capable staff	85.6	69.1	45.3	66.7	81.4	63.2	86.2	76.9

(Table continues on the following page.)

Table 6 (*continued*)

Percentage responses from households under differently managed interventions citing good performance

Function	Karnataka				Madhya Pradesh			
	Swa-Shakthi (N = 257)	*Stree-Shakthi* (N = 220)	*Others* (N = 75)	*Average*	*Swa-Shakthi* (N = 290)	*SGSY* (N = 155)	*Others* (N = 58)	*Average*
Development Oriented								
Coordination with PIA/line department/NGO	73.9	67.7	68.0	69.9	52.4	38.1	51.7	47.4
Training on how to secure benefits for members	71.2	64.5	57.3	64.3	71.0	48.4	74.1	64.5
Organizing training programs and exposure visits	79.4	38.2	32.0	49.9	77.6	51.6	81.0	70.0
Explaining how to improve the habit of savings contributions to local organization	87.5	71.8	38.7	66.0	62.8	41.3	72.4	58.8
Organizing meetings with banks and government departments to obtain assistance for members	61.5	49.5	42.7	51.2	65.9	44.5	63.8	58.1
Training on selecting the right income-generating activities and making them successful	51.8	30.5	41.3	41.2	69.7	38.7	79.3	62.6

Source: Household questionnaire.

Note: NGO = nongovernmental organization; PIA = project implementation agency; and SGSY = Swarnajayanti Gram Swarozgar Yojna.

24

Similar to the findings for support organizations, village-level elected government performance was divided between satisfactory performance of administrative functions and unsatisfactory performance of development-oriented functions in the water supply and sanitation sector (annex tables A11 and A12). In the watershed development sector, GPs were reported to perform few functions well, administrative or development oriented, particularly in Karnataka.[13]

Summary

At the state level, organizations are assigned macrolevel functions necessary for strategic management (staffing and coordination), financing, and maintaining information systems. Elected governments and NGOs are both assigned the most responsibility at the village level, rather than any other level.

In practice, local organizations are often found to delegate assigned functions to subsidiary organizations at lower levels, or to transfer functions among organizations. Functions, however, are performed and the quality of performance generally is reported to be positive. This is particularly the case for performance of administrative and management functions. More development-oriented functions, such as community-based action, capacity building, and information sharing are performed less well. This is particularly true among village-level elected governments.

In an environment in which such a variety of different types of organizations at different levels are assigned such wide-ranging functions, coordination among local organizations is valuable for efficiency and to avoid unnecessary duplication. Coordination committees or multiagency working groups are featured in each sector with such intentions, usually as part of project design. However, few of them were found to function as intended, other than those at the state level in the water and sanitation and watershed sectors and at the district level in the watershed sector. The coordination committees rarely included organizations other than government LDs or government staff of project units, at least in practice, and were generally used more for monitoring purposes than for strategic guidance.

Notes

10. The amount lent by banks to self-help groups (SHGs) stood at 1 percent of total outstanding loans at the time of the survey.

11. In annex table A8, the Advanced Rural Water Supply Program (ARWSP) is labeled as the one managed by gram panchayats (GPs) in Karnataka.

12. Organizational administration and management functions include most subfunctions relating to financing, staffing, provisioning, monitoring and

evaluation, and conflict resolution/accountability. Development functions cover activities aimed at securing resources for the local organization or the beneficiaries, enhancing the capacity of beneficiaries to secure entitlements on the basis of resources or skills possessed, or providing new assets or organizational links to beneficiaries. These functions include most subfunctions related to community-based action, capacity building, coordination, and information sharing/dissemination.

13. Respondents in the women's development sector reported quite limited activity by GPs, and thus ratings of performance quality for these organizations are not provided.

III
Assets and Effective Organizational Performance

The preceding analysis outlined considerable variation in performance of functions among different types of local organizations in the three sectors. The following analysis focuses on the factors associated with different levels of organizational performance. The conceptual framework underpinning this study specifies that an organization's performance is contingent on four groups of factors: its assets, processes, linkages, and context. This section reviews findings on assets and their importance for performance of local organizations. Three types of assets were assessed: human, material, and financial.

Human and Material Assets

Overall, nearly three-quarters of organizations operating at the village level are reported to have adequate human resources (table 7). Just under a quarter of all organizations in the watershed development sector are underresourced with human assets, as are nearly a third of all organizations in the other two sectors. There is some variation by type of organization and state. Excluding the one NGO-VL, in the women's development sector, all types of organizations in Madhya Pradesh are less likely than those in Karnataka to have adequate human resources; in both states the NGO-initiated CBOs are the most poorly endowed. In the water and sanitation sector, LDs operating at the village level are seriously underresourced in Uttaranchal but less so in Karnataka. Sixty-eight percent of GP representatives in Karnataka said they have adequate resources for their work in this sector. In watershed development, organizations in Karnataka were the most poorly endowed in terms of human assets. This was particularly striking for government-initiated CBOs, in which 40 percent of officeholders reported lack of adequate human assets.

Levels of material assets were poorer than those of human assets (table 8). Dissatisfaction was highest for the watershed sector (65 percent), and lowest for the water supply and sanitation sector (55 percent). In the women's development sector, organizations in Madhya Pradesh had far fewer material assets than those in Karnataka and this was true across organizational

Table 7 Adequacy of Human Assets

		Women's development and empowerment sector							
Local organization type	*All*			*Karnataka*			*Madhya Pradesh*		
	No (%)	*Yes (%)*	*N*	*No (%)*	*Yes (%)*	*N*	*No (%)*	*Yes (%)*	*N*
NGO-VL	100	0	1	100	0	1	n.a.	n.a.	n.a.
CBO-GI	22	78	55	12	88	33	36	64	22
CBO-NI	45	55	11	17	83	6	80	20	5
CBO-PI	32	68	60	10	90	30	53	47	30
CBO-SI	50	50	2	n.a.	n.a.	n.a.	50	50	2
Total average[a]	29	71	129	13	87	70	49	51	59

		Drinking water supply and sanitation sector							
Local organization type	*All*			*Karnataka*			*Uttaranchal*		
	No (%)	*Yes (%)*	*N*	*No (%)*	*Yes (%)*	*N*	*No (%)*	*Yes (%)*	*N*
LD	43	57	49	33	67	36	69	31	13
GP	32	68	22	32	68	22	n.a.	n.a.	n.a.
CBO-PI	17	83	58	17	83	29	17	83	29
Total average[a]	29	71	129	28	72	87	33	67	42

		Watershed development sector							
Local organization type	*All*			*Karnataka*			*Uttaranchal*		
	No (%)	*Yes (%)*	*N*	*No (%)*	*Yes (%)*	*N*	*No (%)*	*Yes (%)*	*N*
CBO-GI	44	56	9	60	40	5	25	75	4
CBO-NI	0	100	1	0	100	1	n.a.	n.a.	n.a.
CBO-PI	19	81	59	28	72	29	10	90	30
Total average[a]	22	78	69	31	69	35	12	88	34

Sources: Local organization and GP officials questionnaires.

Note: CBO-GI = community-based organization (government-initiated); CBO-NI = community-based organization (NGO-initiated); CBO-PI = community-based organization (project-initiated); CBO-SI = community-based organization (self-initiated); GP = gram panchayat; LD = line department; NGO-VL = nongovernmental organization (village-level).

n.a. Not applicable (not operating in this sector).

a. Reflects average percentage for all ungrouped organizations.

Table 8 Adequacy of Material Assets

Local organization type	Women's development and empowerment sector								
	All			Karnataka			Madhya Pradesh		
	No (%)	Yes (%)	N	No (%)	Yes (%)	N	No (%)	Yes (%)	N
NGO-VL	0	100	1	0	100	1	n.a.	n.a.	n.a.
CBO-GI	58	42	55	39	61	33	86	14	22
CBO-NI	73	27	11	67	33	6	80	20	5
CBO-PI	59	41	59	30	70	30	90	10	29
CBO-SI	100	0	2	n.a.	n.a.	n.a.	100	0	2
Total average[a]	60	40	128	37	63	70	88	22	58

Local organization type	Drinking water supply and sanitation sector								
	All			Karnataka			Uttaranchal		
	No (%)	Yes (%)	N	No (%)	Yes (%)	N	No (%)	Yes (%)	N
LD	44	56	48	43	57	35	46	54	13
GP	55	45	22	55	45	22	n.a.	n.a.	n.a.
CBO-PI	64	36	58	48	52	29	79	21	29
Total average[a]	55	45	128	48	52	87	69	31	42

Local organization type	Watershed development sector								
	All			Karnataka			Uttaranchal		
	No (%)	Yes (%)	N	No (%)	Yes (%)	N	No (%)	Yes (%)	N
CBO-GI	44	56	9	40	60	5	50	50	4
CBO NI	0	100	1	0	100	1	n.a.	n.a.	n.a.
CBO-PI	69	31	59	45	55	29	93	7	30
Total average[a]	65	35	69	43	57	35	88	12	34

Sources: Local organization and GP officials questionnaires; semistructured interviews with district-level officials.

Note: CBO-GI = community-based organization (government-initiated); CBO-NI = community-based organization (NGO-initiated); CBO-PI = community-based organization (project-initiated); CBO-SI = community-based organization (self-initiated); GP = gram panchayat; LD = line department; NGO-VL = nongovernmental organization (village-level).

n.a. Not applicable (not operating in this sector).

a. Reflects average percentage for all ungrouped organizations.

types. In the drinking water sector, organizations in Uttaranchal had far fewer material assets than those in Karnataka, with project-initiated CBOs suffering particularly badly. Even in Karnataka, however, nearly half of the organizations of this type lacked the material assets that officeholders thought they required, and over half of all GPs reported inadequate material assets. Finally, state differences are again apparent in watershed development, with nearly 90 percent of organizations recording inadequate material assets in Uttaranchal. This difference is particularly apparent for project-initiated CBOs.

Financial Assets

Nearly three-quarters of all organizations working in the women's development sector had insufficient financial assets (table 9). In the water supply and sanitation sector, 6 out of 10 local organizations, and nearly half of all organizations in watershed, reported inadequate financial assets. In the former sector, there was not a great deal of difference between states, but GPs reported severe financial constraints on their work.[14] LDs operating at the village level in Uttaranchal were poorly funded, but to no greater extent than any other local organization in that state.[15]

Summary and Analysis of the Relationship Between Assets and Performance of Functions

Tables 7 through 9 provided an overview of the asset positioning of different organizations. Across sectors, 3 in 10 organizations reported inadequate human assets, 6 in 10 had inadequate material assets, and 7 in 10 had inadequate financial assets. Obviously, the poor asset position of organizations is serious. But is it affecting performance of functions? Table 10 presents ordered probit results on the association between an organization's asset positioning and the quality of performance of the nine main functions.

In terms of human assets, the picture is statistically inconclusive but leaning toward a negative association with performance. In the women's development sector, the number of human assets has no significant relationship with anything other than conflict resolution. In the water supply and sanitation sector, numbers of staff had either insignificant or negative associations with performance of functions. The negative relationship was even more apparent in the watershed sector. Additional staff is obviously not the answer to low quality of performance, but better-quality staff may be (box 3).[16]

The same trend is apparent in the relation between the quantum of material assets available to an organization and its performance. While there is little association between material assets and performance in the water

Table 9 Adequacy of Financial Assets

Women's development and empowerment sector

Local organization type	All			Karnataka			Madhya Pradesh		
	No (%)	Yes (%)	N	No (%)	Yes (%)	N	No (%)	Yes (%)	N
NGO-VL	0	100	1	0	100	1	n.a.	n.a.	n.a.
CBO-GI	76	24	54	64	36	33	95	5	21
CBO-NI	60	40	10	50	50	6	75	25	4
CBO-PI	68	32	59	60	40	30	76	24	29
CBO-SI	100	0	2	n.a.	n.a.	n.a.	100	0	2
Total average[a]	71	29	126	60	40	70	84	16	56

Drinking water supply and sanitation sector

Local organization type	All			Karnataka			Uttaranchal		
	No (%)	Yes (%)	N	No (%)	Yes (%)	N	No (%)	Yes (%)	N
LD	40	60	48	29	71	35	69	31	13
GP	86	14	22	86	14	22	n.a.	n.a.	n.a.
CBO-PI	71	29	58	79	21	29	62	38	29
Total average[a]	62	38	128	60	40	86	64	36	42

Watershed development sector

Local organization type	All			Karnataka			Uttaranchal		
	No (%)	Yes (%)	N	No (%)	Yes (%)	N	No (%)	Yes (%)	N
CBO-GI	63	37	8	40	60	5	100	0	3
CBO-NI	100	0	1	100	0	1	n.a.	n.a.	n.a.
CBO-PI	44	56	59	31	69	29	57	43	30
Total average[a]	47	53	68	34	66	35	61	39	33

Sources: Local organization and GP officials questionnaires.

Note: CBO-GI = community-based organization (government-initiated); CBO-NI = community-based organization (NGO-initiated); CBO-PI = community-based organization (project-initiated); CBO-SI = community-based organization (self-initiated); GP = gram panchayat; LD = line department; NGO-VL = nongovernmental organization (village-level).
n.a. Not applicable (not operating in this sector).
a. Reflects average percentage for all ungrouped organizations.

Table 10 Ordered Probit Results for Assets and Performance

(See annex table A29)

		Function								
Sector	Type of assets	1	2	3	4	5	6	7	8	9
Women	Human assets	o	o	o	o	o	o	o	++	o
	Material assets	o	o	o	-	—	o	o	—	o
	Financial assets	o	o	o	++	o	o	o	o	o
Water/sanitation	Human assets	o	*	-	o	-	-	o	o	o
	Material assets	-	*	o	+	o	o	+	o	o
	Financial assets	++	*	+	o	o	+	o	o	o
Watershed	Human assets	—	-	o	—	—	—	—	—	o
	Material assets	—	o	—	++	—	—	-	-	—
	Financial assets	++	++	++	o	++	++	++	++	++

Sources: Local organization officials and household questionnaires.

Functions: 1 = financing; 2 = staffing; 3 = provisioning; 4 = community-based action; 5 = capacity building; 6 = coordination of activities; 7 = M&E; 8 = conflict resolution; 9 = information sharing/dissemination.
  +   Significant positive association at 95 percent.
++   Significant positive association at 99 percent.
  -   Significant negative association at 95 percent.
—   Significant negative association at 99 percent.
  o   No significant association.
  *   Insufficient data. Relatively few local organizations undertook activities falling under the general function area of staffing. In the case of the drinking water and sanitation projects, in which this problem was particularly acute, this function has not been included in the analysis.

supply and sanitation sector, there is a negative association with development functions in the women's development sector. The same negative relationship is observed with almost all functions in the watershed sector, apart from community-based action. In the last case, the more material assets an organization has, the more likely it is to be effective in terms of generating community-level collective action.

Financial assets have the most significant impact on an organization's performance. In the drinking water and sanitation sector, in which 4 in 10 organizations have sufficient financial assets, these associate positively with financing, provisioning, and external coordination functions. In the watershed sector, where half of all organizations report adequate asset endowments, there is a strong positive relationship with quality of performance of most functions. The relationship is least noticeable in the women's

---

Box 3 Quality of Human Assets Is Key

In the watershed sector, delivery of benefits was linked with contributions. NGO staff played a critical role in motivating farmers to make contributions, and discussions during performance rankings indicated that the benefits to farmers were substantial when the NGO staff carried out this function effectively.

It was reported, however, that NGO staff performance was irregular and some did not undertake the functions assigned to them. For instance, the farmers in S.D. Kote village in Chitradurga stated that the NGO staff had not been providing guidance to farmers on contributions or land development works.

Similar complaints were made in the groups formed by the local administrative government. The president of the watershed committee in Chikkobanahalli stated that the line department staff was irregular, and that works carried out during his tenure were substandard. Furthermore, the committee wanted such works as land leveling, clearing of bushes, and building of checkdams to be taken up. The response of the staff was that "there was shortage of money." The committee resolved in one of its meetings that the staff should be transferred and sent the request to the Department of Agriculture. But the president stated that "no action was taken."

Source: Performance rankings.

---

development sector, in which the only significant association is a positive one with community-based action.

Financial assets are clearly required for good performance. Material and human assets matter less, and interestingly, generally appear to detract from quality of performance. Interventions appear to be unable to provide local organizations with required finance. If local organizations are to succeed, they require higher levels of financial resources. This, along with the issue of local organization resource generation, is discussed further in section VI.

Notes

14. This is consistent with other recent research on fiscal decentralization in Karnataka, which found that local elected governments (from the district level down) had in practice virtually no expenditure discretion in plan funds, as all transfers were already earmarked by state governments. Furthermore, while GPs

were the only elected governments with the authority to generate their own source revenues, because of limited tax collection capacities and weak administrative processes, in 2001 these amounted to less than 1 percent of Gross State Domestic Product. In part because of this, the research found that village-level elected governments "do not evoke appreciable interest and response from the majority of people. Many have commented on the apparent lack of local interest in the business of the *panchayats*, as evidenced by the poor attendance at the *gram sabhas*" (World Bank 2004).

15. In addition to being largely inadequate, sustainability of financial assets of local organizations is also questionable. This is discussed in greater detail in section VI.

16. Analysis of capacity building, organizational business practices, and levels of rules awareness indicates that quality, rather than number, of staff may be significant (Alsop 2004). It is essential to ensure that organizational staff have sufficient knowledge and skills to perform the tasks required of them. This requires immediate attention in interventions under implementation, as well as enhanced capacity-building strategies for staff and functionaries in the design of future projects.

IV

Processes and Effective
Organizational Performance

Processes refer to the manner in which a local organization engages its beneficiaries and, to a lesser extent, other stakeholders. Believing them to be core to the functioning of democratic organizations, project designers have encouraged local organizations to operate in a transparent and participatory manner. This is understood to improve functional performance and lead to better equity outcomes. Furthermore, such organizations are thought to be more likely to be sustainable beyond the life of a project.

This section reviews the extent to which local organizations in the sectors studied carry out such processes in practice, and the extent to which such processes impact performance. Descriptive statistics for key variables are first presented, followed by discussion of regression estimations of the association between organizational processes and the quality of the organizations' performance of functions. Key indicators used to investigate how a group manages itself and its business include levels of awareness of organizational rules, transparency of operation, and decision-making procedures.

Awareness of Rules

Tables 11 and 12 show the levels of awareness representatives and members have of rules across sectors and types of organization. A full awareness of rules is rare, as is having no awareness of rules at all. Overall, around half of all CBO representatives are aware of some of their organization's rules (table 13).

Awareness among representatives is highest for project-initiated CBOs and lowest for government-initiated CBOs, where in all sectors, around 30 percent had no knowledge of organizational rules. At least 13 percent of representatives of project-initiated CBOs had no knowledge of organizational rules. In the women's development and water supply and sanitation sectors, this figure approached 20 percent, but it was far lower (2 percent) for watershed interventions. In the drinking water sector, among representatives of LDs, 18 percent had no knowledge of the rules governing their operation. Just under 10 percent of GP representatives admitted they had no knowledge of the rules governing the GP's involvement in this sector.

Table 11 Representatives' Awareness of Rules and Functions, by Local Organization Type and Sector

(percent)

Local organization type	All				Women				Water/sanitation				Watershed			
	None	Some	All	N	None	Some	All	N	None	Some	All	N	None	Some	All	N
Admin. Govt.	18	73	9	11	n.a.	n.a.	n.a.	n.a.	18	73	9	11	n.a.	n.a.	n.a.	n.a.
Elected Govt.	9	69	22	23	n.a.	n.a.	n.a.	n.a.	9	69	22	23	n.a.	n.a.	n.a.	n.a.
NGO-VL	0	100	0	1	0	100	0	1	n.a.	n.a.	n.a.	n.a.	n.a.	n.a.	n.a.	n.a.
CBO-GI	30	45	25	64	29	49	22	55	n.a.	n.a.	n.a.	n.a.	33	22	44	9
CBO-NI	25	58	17	12	27	64	9	11	n.a.	n.a.	n.a.	n.a.	0	0	100	1
CBO-PI	13	56	31	175	17	62	21	58	19	41	40	58	2	66	32	59
CBO-SI	0	50	50	2	0	50	50	2	n.a.	n.a.	n.a.	n.a.	n.a.	n.a.	n.a.	n.a.
Average across all orgs.	17	56	27	288	23	57	20	127	16	52	32	92	6	59	35	69

Source: Local organization officials questionnaire.

Note: CBO-GI = community-based organization (government-initiated); CBO-NI = community-based organization (NGO-initiated); CBO-PI = community-based organization (project-initiated); CBO-SI = community-based organization (self-initiated); NGO-VL = nongovernmental organization (village-level).

n.a. Not applicable.

Table 12 Members' Awareness of Rules, by Local Organization Type and Sector

Local organization type	All			Women			Water/sanitation			Watershed		
	No (%)	Yes (%)	N	No (%)	Yes (%)	N	No (%)	Yes (%)	N	No (%)	Yes (%)	N
Elected Govt.	30	70	23	n.a.	n.a.	n.a.	30	70	23	n.a.	n.a.	n.a.
NGO	0	100	1	0	100	1	n.a.	n.a.	n.a.	n.a.	n.a.	n.a.
CBO-GI	39	61	64	36	64	55	n.a.	n.a.	n.a.	56	44	9
CBO-NI	33	67	12	36	64	11	n.a.	n.a.	n.a.	0	100	1
CBO-PI	22	78	176	22	78	59	24	76	58	19	81	59
CBO-SI	0	100	2	0	100	2	n.a.	n.a.	n.a.	n.a.	n.a.	n.a.
Average across all orgs.	26	74	289	29	71	128	23	77	92	23	77	69

Source: Local organization officials questionnaire.

Note: CBO-GI = community-based organization (government-initiated); CBO-NI = community-based organization (NGO-initiated); CBO-PI = community-based organization (project-initiated); CBO-SI = community-based organization (self-initiated); NGO = nongovernmental organization.

n.a. Not applicable.

The proportion of members unaware of organizational rules was higher (table 12). Overall, nearly one-third of members of women's groups and one-quarter of members in the water supply and sanitation and watershed sectors were unaware of organizational rules. Similar to the findings for representatives' awareness, project-initiated CBOs have the best record of members' awareness and government-initiated CBOs the worst.

Transparency and Information Availability

As indicated by the reports in box 4, transparency plays an important role in enhancing the quality of an organization's performance. Sharing minutes from previous meetings is a key transparency mechanism.

In addition to updating members who missed the preceding meeting, reading minutes allows an organization's members to verify records and to reopen discussion on matters dealt with previously. Table 13, which presents findings on the reading of minutes at meetings, suggests that this practice is far from universal. Minutes are read, on average, at the meetings of 60 percent of organizations across sectors. This is lowest in the water supply and sanitation sector, in which 58 percent of organizations do not read minutes. This largely results from low incidence among administrative and elected governments, who read minutes in only 8 and 30 percent of cases, respectively. Performance is better, but still somewhat low, in the watershed and women's development sectors, in which minutes are read in 75 percent and 65 percent of organizations respectively. Project-initiated CBOs in all sectors have the best record, but even then more than one-quarter do not use this transparency mechanism.

As later analysis shows (table 28) attendance at meetings of local organizations is low, so what mechanisms exist that allow members not present at a meeting to learn what happened? As table 14 shows, many organizations rely on word of mouth for transmitting information about the activities and decisions that take place when an organization meets. This is especially the case among NGOs and CBOs in all sectors. Word of mouth, while common, is a mode of information sharing in which messages are frequently subject to different interpretations. It can also be selectively used. In general, CBOs place too much reliance on this highly unreliable mechanism for sharing information among members. Unless backed by available records of meetings, this practice renders organizations vulnerable to mismanagement, as box 5 demonstrates.

Because of its key role in good governance, transparency is critical to organizational sustainability. Women's development organizations appear the least likely to suffer from future problems. In general, however, organizations across sectors do not appear to prioritize transparency of operation. This obviously requires those designing interventions to pay more

Box 4 Transparency in Operation—or Not

The members of Swa-Shakthi and Swarnajayanti Gram Swarozgar Yojna (SGSY) groups in Madhya Pradesh did not consider it necessary to know the annual income and expenditure of their groups. For instance, two members of the Swa-Shakthi group of Nayagaon village in Chattarpur district stated that "the secretary of the group should know this" and said they only kept track of their own money in the group. Swa-Shakthi group members in Dadudhana village in Betul reported that "the information on income and expenditure is known to only some influential persons who are actively involved in the group." In some villages, such as Raipur village in Betul district, an "annual budget was never prepared and discussed."

It was alleged that the support organizations, which trained the groups to be transparent, were themselves not transparent. The members of the self-help group in Raipur village noted that individual savings passbooks were not provided, savings records were not up-to-date, and members did not have information on the total savings and their own savings in the group.

Members also complained about lack of transparency with regard to the distribution of benefits. One of the Stree-Shakthi members from Maradaghatta village, who belonged to the scheduled-caste (SC) community, noted that the president (upper caste), vice-president (SC), and anganawadi worker accounted for more than one-third of the total loans from the group. She stated that the criteria for distribution of benefits were not clear. She also hinted that the decision-making process was not made transparent to members belonging to the lower castes.

In the watershed sector, transparency norms also proved nonfunctional. Gram Resources Management Associations (GAREMAs) in six sample villages were provided with agricultural assets such as sprayers. While these were used to meet the requirements of farmers in a few villages, they were misused in several cases. In Gajpur village of Ramnagar block in Nainital district, the project had provided the GAREMA with a sprayer for the villagers to use. However, the people did not know this. The president of the GAREMA, a local landlord with around 40 acres of land, had taken custody of the sprayer, apparently for his own use. The general public had no idea the sprayer was available for rent, and the watershed committee therefore lost a means of generating income.

Source: Case studies.

Table 13 Meeting Minutes Read, by Local Organization Type and Sector

Local organization type	All			Women			Water/sanitation			Watershed		
	No (%)	Yes (%)	N	No (%)	Yes (%)	N	No (%)	Yes (%)	N	No (%)	Yes (%)	N
Admin. Govt.	92	8	331	n.a.	n.a.	n.a.	92	8	331	n.a.	n.a.	n.a.
Elected Govt.	70	30	117	n.a.	n.a.	n.a.	70	30	117	n.a.	n.a.	n.a.
NGO	100	0	4	100	0	4	n.a.	n.a.	n.a.	n.a.	n.a.	n.a.
CBO-GI	40	60	556	47	53	392	n.a.	n.a.	n.a.	22	78	174
CBO-NI	43	57	87	39	61	71	n.a.	n.a.	n.a.	56	44	16
CBO-PI	30	70	2,079	26	74	539	40	60	666	25	75	874
CBO-SI	0	100	22	0	100	22	n.a.	n.a.	n.a.	n.a.	n.a.	n.a.
Average across all orgs.	40	60	3,206	35	65	1,028	58	42	1,114	25	75	1,064

Source: Household questionnaire.

Note: CBO-GI = community-based organization (government-initiated); CBO-NI = community-based organization (NGO-initiated); CBO-PI = community-based organization (project-initiated); CBO-SI = community-based organization (self-initiated); NGO = nongovernmental organization. n.a. Not applicable.

Table 14 Meeting Information through Word of Mouth, by Local Organization Type and Sector

Local organization type	All			Women			Water/sanitation			Watershed		
	No (%)	Yes (%)	N	Nc (%)	Yes (%)	N	No (%)	Yes (%)	N	No (%)	Yes (%)	N
Admin. Govt.	78	22	328	n.a.	n.a.	n.a.	78	22	328	n.a.	n.a.	n.a.
Elected Govt.	43	57	119	n.a.	n.a.	n.a.	43	57	119	n.a.	n.a.	n.a.
NGO	0	100	4	0	100	4	n.a.	n.a.	n.a.	n.a.	n.a.	n.a.
CBO-GI	17	83	565	15	85	391	n.a.	n.a.	n.a.	21	79	174
CBO-NI	31	69	87	28	72	71	n.a.	n.a.	n.a.	44	56	16
CBO-PI	15	85	2,074	10	90	539	23	77	662	11	89	873
CBO-SI	5	95	22	5	95	22	n.a.	n.a.	n.a.	n.a.	n.a.	n.a.
Average across all orgs.	23	77	3,199	13	87	1,028	42	58	1,109	13	87	1,063

Source: Household questionnaire.

Note: CBO-GI = community-based organization (government-initiated); CBO-NI = community-based organization (NGO-initiated); CBO-PI = community-based organization (project-initiated); CBO-SI = community-based organization (self-initiated); NGO = nongovernmental organization.

n.a. Not applicable.

Box 5 The Importance of Good Transparency Mechanisms

In one of the villages studied, the community organizer helped a women's self-help group to establish linkages with a local commercial bank. After the financial assistance was approved for the group, the community organizer stated that each member would have to pay Rs 200 toward the expenses incurred by the bankers. However, she showed no proof of this requirement. The group members paid up and the bank loans were disbursed. But the president of the group became suspicious and sent her husband to check this with the manager of the bank branch, who stated that no such amount was requested or obtained from the members. The group members asked for an explanation from the community organizer and made her return their money. They also pressed for the removal of the community organizer. The NGO transferred her to another area, and appointed a fresh graduate to the position, after a delay of about three months. The NGO confirmed this incident, and stated that action was taken against the staff member concerned.

There were also three instances of Stree-Shakthi staff using the members' savings for their personal gain. Because banks were not located in these villages, it was the practice for the anganawadi worker to deposit members' savings in the banks. This resulted in members losing trust, and their gradual withdrawal from the group.

Source: Performance ranking.

---

attention both to the establishment of transparency measures and to monitoring their use.

Decision-Making Procedures

Participation in collective decision making is argued to be a necessary condition for equitable and sustainable development outcomes. Such participation is seen as ensuring that the interests of marginalized groups are voiced and considered, that all participants accept responsibility for the decisions made, and that the subsequent activities undertaken are collectively owned. Collective decision making is expected to lead to better distribution of benefits (greater equity) and to increase people's motivation to engage in local governance and development. Some of the factors that come into play when trying to achieve these objectives are highlighted in box 6.

The mode of decision-making processes varies widely by sector. Table 15 shows how key decisions are reached in organizations in the women's

---

Box 6 Elite Capture

In Jigjeevani in Bijapur district in Karnataka, the NGO staff preferred to have the local landlord as a representative, because his support was considered useful to the NGO for carrying out watershed works in the village. Similarly, influence of the local elite in the election of officeholders was evident in Inderpur, a village in Nainital district with many well-off farmers. The president of the Gram Resources Management Associations (GAREMA), in view of his dominant position in the locality, became the leader of the organization and has continued to hold the position since inception.

In many other villages as well—such as Gajpur, Bhalon, and Dharamgarh in Uttaranchal, to name just a few—the officeholders of the GAREMA came from the local elite. They were local landlords, retired army personnel, and the like, who became officeholders because of their status in their village. Village-level project staff went along with this as it ensured that they could carry out their activities with the blessings of, or at least without much opposition from, powerful local citizens.

Source: Focus group discussion.

---

development sector—by secret majority vote, by general consensus, or by the local organization president. The overwhelming majority of respondents stated that decision making in their organization was by general consensus. This is less so but still largely the case in the watershed development sector (table 16). In the drinking water supply and sanitation sector, by contrast, only 54 percent of respondents report at least partial consensus in decision making, and 23 percent report that there is no consensus at all (table 17).

Who participates in decision making is another key question. This question is taken up in detail in section VI, in which equity of organizational performance is discussed.

Relationship Between Processes and Performance of Functions

Analysis of organizational processes intended to ensure inclusiveness of stakeholders suggests a need for improvement across sectors. Full awareness of organizational rules and functions among both members *and* representatives appears to be rare, with the exception of the water and sanitation sector, in which awareness among both is relatively high.

Table 15 How Decisions Are Made, Women's Development and Empowerment Sector

Local organization type	Secret majority vote (%)	General consensus (%)	Local organization president (%)	Other (%)	N
All					
NGO	0	100	0	0	4
CBO-GI	1	91	4	4	399
CBO-NI	0	92	4	4	70
CBO-PI	0	96	3	1	544
CBO-SI	0	86	0	14	22
Average across all orgs.	1	94	3	2	1,039
Karnataka					
NGO	0	100	0	0	4
CBO-GI	1	90	6	4	248
CBO-NI	0	86	7	7	43
CBO-PI	0	95	5	0	257
CBO-SI	n.a.	n.a.	n.a.	n.a.	n.a.
Average across all orgs.	1	92	5	2	552
Madhya Pradesh					
NGO	n.a.	n.a.	n.a.	n.a.	n.a.
CBO-GI	0	93	3	6	151
CBO-NI	0	100	0	0	27
CBO-PI	0	98	1	1	287
CBO-SI	0	86	0	14	22
Average across all orgs.	0	96	1	3	487

Source: Household questionnaire.

Note: CBO-GI = community-based organization (government-initiated); CBO-NI = community-based organization (NGO-initiated); CBO-PI = community-based organization (project-initiated); CBO-SI = community-based organization (self-initiated); NGO = nongovernmental organization.

n.a. Not applicable.

Table 16 Extent to Which Decisions Are Made by Consensus, Watershed Development Sector
(Percent)

Local organization type	All					Karnataka					Uttaranchal				
	Do not know	Not at all	Partially	To a large extent	N	Do not know	Not at all	Partially	To a large extent	N	Do not know	Not at all	Partially	To a large extent	N
CBO-GI	3	6	6	85	173	0	10	1	89	80	5	3	10	82	93
CBO-NI	6	19	6	69	16	6	19	6	69	16	n.a.	n.a.	n.a.	n.a.	n.a.
CBO-PI	5	3	5	87	879	1	2	6	91	455	9	5	3	83	424
Average across all orgs.	5	4	5	86	1,068	1	4	5	90	551	9	4	4	82	517

Source: Household questionnaire.

Note: CBO-GI = community-based organization (government-initiated); CBO-NI = community-based organization (NGO-initiated); CBO-PI = community-based organization (project-initiated).
n.a. Not applicable.

Table 17 Extent to Which Decisions Are Made by Consensus, Drinking Water Supply and Sanitation Sector

(Percent)

Local organization type	All					Karnataka					Uttaranchal				
	Do not know	Not at all	Partially	To a large extent	N	Do not know	Not at all	Partially	To a large extent	N	Do not know	Not at all	Partially	To a large extent	N
LD-VL	42	41	3	14	327	10	63	5	22	210	99	1	0	0	117
GP	11	56	3	30	123	11	56	3	30	123	n.a.	n.a.	n.a.	n.a.	n.a.
CBO-PI	16	8	13	63	676	31	19	9	41	240	7	2	15	76	436
Average across all orgs.	23	23	9	45	1,126	19	43	7	31	573	27	2	11	60	553

Source: Household questionnaire.

Note: CBO-PI = community-based organization (project-initiated); GP = gram panchayat; LD-VL = line department (village-level). n.a. Not applicable.

Organizational transparency is also of concern, with heavy reliance across sectors on word of mouth for transferring meeting information, which leaves organizations open to mismanagement as this information can be unreliable. More transparent means of information dissemination, such as reading meeting minutes aloud, are much less prominent, and particularly low in the water and sanitation sector.

How do organizational processes impact their performance of functions? Table 18 presents ordered probit results on the extent of association between an organization's processes and its performance of functions. Broadly, findings indicate that the relative impact of organizational processes on performance depends on sector and type of organization.

- *Members' awareness of rules* shows a positive relationship with a number of functions in the women's development sector and the water supply and sanitation sector. But it has negative associations with several functions in watershed, including staffing, community-based action, conflict resolution, and information sharing.
- *Representatives' awareness of rules* is generally positively associated with performance in women's development and watershed, but it has an overall negative relationship with performance in water supply and sanitation. Organization members in this sector report little belief in accountability practices or rules, whereas in the other sectors the accountability rules, while still not properly functioning, were used more frequently.[17]
- *Oral transmission of information* associates with poor performance in financing and staffing for the women's development sector, but it has no significant association with performance in the water supply and sanitation sector and a positive relationship with performance in watershed. For women's groups, because many SHG members are illiterate, oral transmission of business transactions is important. Given the susceptibility of this form of information sharing to misinterpretation, better use should be made of mechanisms, such as reading minutes, which reinforce information about financing and staffing.
- At the same time, however, currently the only significant finding in relation to *reading minutes* is in the water supply and sanitation sector, in which there is a positive association with conflict resolution. There are no negative associations with this practice. This suggests that while such an activity has no statistical association with organizational performance, in the interests of due process it is worth continuing.
- In the women's development sector, the greater the *availability of minutes by request* the poorer an organization performs its financing and, interestingly, its information-sharing and dissemination role. In the watershed sector, the availability of minutes on request is more likely to be found in organizations that perform community-based action and capacity

Table 18 Ordered Probit Results for Processes and Performance

(See annex table A29)

Sector	Attribute	Function								
		1	*2*	*3*	*4*	*5*	*6*	*7*	*8*	*9*
Women	Always conducts self-monitoring	o	o	o	o	+	o	o	o	o
	Members aware of objectives	o	o	+	o	+	o	o	o	o
	Meeting minutes read	o	o	o	o	o	o	o	o	o
	Members aware of rules	+	o	++	o	++	+	o	o	++
	Representatives aware of rules	o	o	++	+	++	+	o	o	++
	Meeting minutes orally informed	− −	-	o	o	o	o	o	o	++
	Minutes available on request	-	o	o	o	o	o	o	o	− −
Water/sanitation	Always conducts self-monitoring	-	*	o	-	− −	− −	o	o	o
	Members aware of objectives	++	*	++	+	− −	o	− −	o	++
	Meeting minutes read	o	*	++	o	o	++	o	++	o
	Members aware of rules	o	*	++	o	++	++	++	++	o
	Representatives aware of rules	o	*	− −	− −	− −	o	− −	− −	-
	Meeting minutes orally informed	o	*	o	o	o	o	o	o	o
	Minutes available on request	o	*	o	o	o	o	o	o	o

Watershed	1	2	3	4	5	6	7	8	9
Always conducts self-monitoring	+	o	++	++	++	o	++	++	++
Members aware of objectives	o	-	o	++	++	-	o	—	o
Meeting minutes read	o	o	o	o	o	o	o	o	o
Members aware of rules	o	—	o	—	o	++	o	-	—
Representatives aware of rules	o	o	+	o	o	++	o	o	++
Meeting minutes orally informed	o	o	++	++	++	+	++	++	o
Minutes available on request	o	o	o	-	—	o	o	o	o

Sources: Local organization officials and household questionnaires.

Functions: 1 = financing; 2 = staffing; 3 = provisioning; 4 = community-based action; 5 = capacity building; 6 = coordination of activities; 7 = M&E; 8 = conflict resolution; 9 = information sharing/dissemination.

+ Significant positive association at 95 percent.
++ Significant positive association at 99 percent.
- Significant negative association at 95 percent.
— Significant negative association at 99 percent.
o No significant association.
* Insufficient data. Relatively few local organizations undertook activities falling under the general function area of staffing. In the case of the drinking water and sanitation projects, in which this problem was particularly acute, this function has not been included in the analysis.

building functions poorly. In the water supply and sanitation sector, there are no significant associations. These findings suggest that, at the current level of evolution of organizations in most sectors, availability of minutes is not critical. However, as organizations move forward into independent and perhaps more sophisticated action, other research demonstrates that this transparency mechanism will become increasingly important.

Note

17. In the water and sanitation sector, only 17 percent of households in Karnataka and 5 percent in Uttaranchal had complained about poorly functioning water resources. In the watershed development sector more than 60 percent of organizations had functioning complaint systems. In Karnataka, all complaints were dealt with. In Uttaranchal, one-fifth were not. Figures and effectiveness varied by intervention in women's development and empowerment but, on average, more than half of all organizations had functioning complaint systems and only about 15 percent of complaints were not attended to (Alsop 2004, volume 3, parts 2, 4, 6).

V
Linkages, Context, and Effective Organizational Performance

Two additional factors are held to influence the performance of organizations at the local level: linkages with other local organizations, and the context in which those organizations operate. These are considered in turn in this section.

Linkages

A dense network of linkages is often associated with higher levels of performance of an organization and to better development outcomes for individuals. The significance of three specific linkages for performance of functions by local organizations is assessed here: local organization's linkages with village-level elected governments; with other local organizations, ranging from village to district levels; and with LDs. Linkages are first assessed descriptively and then regression analysis is used to identify significant associations between the linkages an organization has and its quality of performance of the nine major functions.

Linkages with Village-Level Elected Governments

Linkages with elected government at the village level vary by sector and by organizational type, but are generally high. Half of the local organizations in the women's development sector, nearly 80 percent in the water and sanitation sector, and just over 70 percent in the watershed sector have linkages with GPs (table 19).

In the women's development sector, in which linkages are fewest, project-initiated CBOs are more likely to link with GPs than any other CBO. The relationship is slightly more common in Madhya Pradesh than in Karnataka. In the water supply and sanitation sector, administrative government bodies always link with elected governments in Karnataka, but seldom do in Uttaranchal. In Karnataka, all project-initiated CBOs connect to elected governments, but in Uttaranchal the figure is lower at 66 percent. In the watershed sector, in which three-quarters of all organizations link to GPs, figures are higher in Karnataka than in Uttaranchal.

Table 19 Organizational Linkages with Elected Government

Local organization type	Women's development and empowerment sector								
	All			Karnataka			Madhya Pradesh		
	No (%)	Yes (%)	N	No (%)	Yes (%)	N	No (%)	Yes (%)	N
NGO-VL	100	0	1	100	0	1	n.a.	n.a.	n.a.
CBO-GI	55	45	56	59	41	34	50	50	22
CBO-NI	83	17	12	86	14	7	80	20	5
CBO-PI	40	60	60	43	57	30	37	63	30
CBO-SI	100	0	2	n.a.	n.a.	n.a.	100	0	2
Total average[a]	52	48	131	56	44	72	47	53	59

Local organization type	Drinking water supply and sanitation sector								
	All			Karnataka			Uttaranchal		
	No (%)	Yes (%)	N	No (%)	Yes (%)	N	No (%)	Yes (%)	N
Admin. Gov't.	20	80	50	0	100	36	71	29	14
CBO-PI	17	83	59	0	100	30	34	66	29
Total average[a]	23	77	109	0	100	66	47	53	43

Local organization type	Watershed development sector								
	All			Karnataka			Uttaranchal		
	No (%)	Yes (%)	N	No (%)	Yes (%)	N	No (%)	Yes (%)	N
CBO-GI	40	60	10	0	100	5	80	20	5
CBO-NI	0	100	1	0	100	1	n.a.	n.a.	n.a.
CBO-PI	25	75	59	17	83	29	33	67	30
Total average[a]	27	73	70	14	86	35	40	60	35

Source: Organizational mapping.

Note: CBO-GI = community-based organization (government-initiated); CBO-NI = community-based organization (NGO-initiated); CBO-PI = community-based organization (project-initiated); CBO-SI = community-based organization (self-initiated); NGO-VL = nongovernmental organization (village-level).
n.a. Not applicable (not operating in this sector).
a. Reflects average percentage for all ungrouped organizations.

Linkages with Administrative Government

In terms of linkages with administrative government bodies, there are differences among sectors (table 20). Nearly three-quarters of organizations in the water supply and sanitation sector, including all organizations

Table 20 Organizational Linkages with Line Departments

Women's development and empowerment sector								
Local organization type	All			Karnataka			Madhya Pradesh		
	No (%)	Yes (%)	N	No (%)	Yes (%)	N	No (%)	Yes (%)	N
NGO-VL	100	0	1	100	0	1	n.a.	n.a.	n.a.
CBO-GI	82	18	56	76	24	34	91	9	22
CBO-NI	92	8	12	86	14	7	100	0	5
CBO-PI	93	7	60	87	13	30	100	0	30
CBO-SI	100	0	2	n.a.	n.a.	n.a.	100	0	2
Total average[a]	89	11	131	82	18	72	97	3	59

Drinking water supply and sanitation sector								
Local organization type	All			Karnataka			Uttaranchal		
	No (%)	Yes (%)	N	No (%)	Yes (%)	N	No (%)	Yes (%)	N
Elected govt.	0	100	25	0	100	25	n.a.	n.a.	n.a.
CBO-PI	41	59	58	0	100	30	86	14	28
Total average[a]	28	72	83	0	100	55	86	14	28

Watershed development sector								
Local organization type	All			Karnataka			Uttaranchal		
	No (%)	Yes (%)	N	No (%)	Yes (%)	N	No (%)	Yes (%)	N
CBO-GI	60	40	10	40	60	5	80	20	5
CBO-NI	0	100	1	0	100	1	n.a.	n.a.	n.a.
CBO-PI	76	24	59	66	34	29	87	13	30
Total average[a]	73	27	70	60	40	35	86	14	35

Source: Organizational mapping.

Note: CBO-GI = community-based organization (government-initiated); CBO-NI = community-based organization (NGO-initiated); CBO-PI = community-based organization (project-initiated); CBO-SI = community-based organization (self-initiated); NGO-VL = nongovernmental organization (village-level).
n.a. Not applicable (not operating in this sector).
a. Reflects average percentage for all ungrouped organizations.

in Karnataka, have linkages to line agencies. In the watershed sector, however, just over 25 percent of organizations have linkages to LDs, and in the women's development sector, figures are much lower at only 11 percent overall.

Linkages with Other Local Organizations in a Sector

As box 7 illustrates, linkages among local organizations within a sector can have multiple and important effects. Table 21 shows sector and state differences in the extent to which linkages are formed with sector local organizations, other than elected and administrative government bodies. Overall linkages with other local organizations are less common than those with

---

Box 7 The Importance of Group-to-Group Linkages

Kerekondapura in Chitradurga district is a multicaste village with the Lingayat community in a dominant position both numerically and economically. A majority of the scheduled-caste households (the second-largest community) are landless laborers and marginal and small farmers. The village is relatively developed, with a good access road, connections with the outside world, public infrastructure, cultivation of cash crops, and marketing facilities.

A Swa-Shakthi women's group was formed in 2000 with 20 members, most of them from the Lingayat community. The group did well in attending meetings, contributing savings, borrowing, and repayment. The members took loans for tailoring, purchasing cows and sheep, vegetable trading, petty business ventures such as tea stalls, and consumption purposes such as home repair and education. The members even tried to undertake nontraditional activities such as stitching jeans and other garments, food processing, and so forth.

A Stree-Shakthi group was formed in the same village in 2000. All the members belonged to scheduled castes and scheduled tribes. The members stated that they had learned from the Swa-Shakthi group about the importance of regular attendance and savings. Although there had been drought in the area for the last couple of years, the members had been saving regularly and had obtained bank assistance. All the members had taken loans, which were used only for health and consumption. Although repayment had been nil because of members' lack of regular employment and the impact of drought on their livelihoods, they continued to contribute savings. The members said, "You see how the other group is functioning. If we cannot function as well as the other group does, we should at least regularly contribute savings. Otherwise, we will be the laughingstock of the village. Whatever may be our problem, we should continue to function."

Source: Focus group discussions.

Table 21 Organizational Linkages with Other Sector Local Organizations

	Women's development and empowerment sector								
Local organization type	All			Karnataka			Madhya Pradesh		
	No (%)	Yes (%)	N	No (%)	Yes (%)	N	No (%)	Yes (%)	N
NGO-VL	100	0	1	100	0	1	n.a.	n.a.	n.a.
CBO-GI	65	35	55	55	45	33	82	18	22
CBO-NI	42	58	12	29	71	7	60	40	5
CBO-PI	52	48	60	43	57	30	60	40	30
CBO-SI	50	50	2	n.a.	n.a.	n.a.	50	50	2
Total average[a]	57	43	130	48	52	71	68	32	59

	Drinking water supply and sanitation sector								
Local organization type	All			Karnataka			Uttaranchal		
	No (%)	Yes (%)	N	No (%)	Yes (%)	N	No (%)	Yes (%)	N
LD	29	71	48	6	94	36	100	0	12
GP	16	84	25	16	84	25	n.a.	n.a.	n.a.
CBO-PI	59	41	58	30	70	30	90	11	28
Total average[a]	40	60	131	16	84	91	93	7	40

	Watershed development sector								
Local organization type	All			Karnataka			Uttaranchal		
	No (%)	Yes (%)	N	No (%)	Yes (%)	N	No (%)	Yes (%)	N
CBO-GI	80	20	10	60	40	5	100	0	5
CBO-NI	100	0	1	100	0	1	n.a.	n.a.	n.a.
CBO-PI	69	31	59	59	41	29	80	20	30
Total average[a]	71	29	70	60	40	35	83	17	35

Source: Organizational mapping.
n.a. Not applicable (not operating in this sector).
Note: Covers organizations other than GPs and line agencies. CBO-GI = community-based organization (government-initiated); CBO-NI = community-based organization (NGO-initiated); CBO-PI = community-based organization (project-initiated); CBO-SI = community-based organization (self-initiated); GP = gram panchayat; LD = line department; NGO-VL = nongovernmental organization (village-level).
a. Reflects average percentage for all ungrouped organizations.

elected government, but slightly more so than with administrative government. The water supply and sanitation sector has the highest rate, with about 60 percent of organizations having such linkages. The corresponding figures are approximately 30 percent for the watershed sector and just over 40 percent for the women's development sector. In the latter sector, more organizational linkages are present for local organizations operating in Karnataka than in Madhya Pradesh.

In the water supply and sanitation sector very few organizations demonstrate linkages with other organizations in Uttaranchal, whereas in Karnataka more than 80 percent have such linkages. In the watershed sector, organizations in Uttaranchal are rather unlikely to link with other organizations, while in Karnataka 40 percent do so.

Relationship Between Linkages and Performance of Functions

Do linkages among local organizations influence their performance of functions? Table 22 presents findings from regression analysis by sector and state. Looking first at linkages with administrative government bodies across sectors, the results indicate that line agencies are not, at present, providing any real assistance to rural women's development and empowerment groups. Where such linkages exist in Karnataka, this relationship has a negative association with the quality of provisioning, community-based action, and capacity building. In Madhya Pradesh, this linkage associates with poor financing performance. In the drinking water and sanitation sector, linkages with LDs associate positively with conflict resolution and information sharing, but negatively with financing and community-based action.[18]

Administrative government linkages have significant positive associations with most functions in the watershed sector. This is particularly noticeable in Uttaranchal, where these linkages associate with good performance in all functions except for information sharing—and even here the association is only indifferent. While less pronounced in Karnataka, the relationship between local organizations and LDs associates positively with staffing, financing, capacity building, and information sharing.

Linkages with village-level elected governments associate with mixed results. In the women's sector, this relationship in Madhya Pradesh associates with poor provisioning and good capacity building, while in Karnataka it associates with good community-based action and capacity building. In the water supply and sanitation sector there is a negative association between linkages with GPs and performance in provisioning, community-based action, and conflict resolution. However, these linkages associate strongly with good capacity building. For watershed organizations, linkages with GPs in both Karnataka and Uttaranchal have a negative association with performance of most functions.

Table 22 Ordered Probit Results for Linkages and Performance

(See annex table A32)

Sector	Links with				Function					
		1	2	3	4	5	6	7	8	9
Women	Gram panchayats (Karnataka)	o	o	o	++	+	o	o	o	o
	Gram panchayats (Madhya Pradesh)	o	o	—	o	o	o	o	o	o
	Other local organizations (Karnataka)	+	o	++	o	++	o	++	++	o
	Other local organizations (Madhya Pradesh)	o	+	o	o	o	o	-	o	o
	Line department (Karnataka)	o	*	—	-	-	o	+	o	+
	Line department (Madhya Pradesh)	—	*	o	o	o	o	o	o	o
Water/sanitation	Gram panchayats	o	*	—	-	++	o	o	—	o
	Other local organizations	o	*	o	o	o	+	++	o	o
	Line department	-	*	o	—	o	o	o	++	++

(Table continues on the following page.)

Table 22 (*continued*)

Sector	Links with	Function								
		1	2	3	4	5	6	7	8	9
Watershed	Gram panchayats (Karnataka)	o	o	—	o	—	-	o	o	—
	Gram panchayats (Uttaranchal)	o	+	-	o	—	—	o	++	—
	Other local organizations (Karnataka)	o	o	—	o	o	+	o	o	-
	Other local organizations (Uttaranchal)	—	-	o	—	—	-	—	-	o
	Line department (Karnataka)	+	++	o	o	++	o	o	o	+
	Line department (Uttaranchal)	++	++	++	++	++	++	++	++	o

Sources: Local organization officials and household questionnaires.

Functions: 1 = financing; 2 = staffing; 3 = provisioning; 4 = community-based action; 5 = capacity building; 6 = coordination of activities; 7 = M&E; 8 = conflict resolution/accountability; 9 = information sharing/dissemination.

+ Significant positive association at 95 percent.
++ Significant positive association at 99 percent.
- Significant negative association at 95 percent.
— Significant negative association at 99 percent.
o No significant association.
* Insufficient data. Relatively few local organizations undertook activities falling under the general function area of staffing. In the case of the drinking water and sanitation projects, in which this problem was particularly acute, this function has not been included in the analysis.

In relation to other sector organizations, positive associations are particularly strong for women's organizations in Karnataka, but less so in Madhya Pradesh, where only staffing improves with an increased number of linkages and M&E actually deteriorates. This finding raises interesting questions about the value of federating women's SHGs—a cornerstone of much of the work in this sector, which requires more investigation. In the water and sanitation sector, linkages with other organizations have a positive association with external coordination and M&E. In the watershed sector, linkages to other organizations primarily have a negative or indifferent impact on performance.

Context

Two clusters of variables are used to test the importance of context to organizational performance. The first cluster, which focuses on the internal environment of the organization, concerns attributes of member households and includes household caste, poverty ranking, landholding, gender of household head, and the respondent's meeting attendance. The second cluster focuses on the external environment in which an organization operates and considers a range of village attributes, the sector in which an organization is located, and the state in which the study took place.

Internal Environment

Looking first at member characteristics in the women's development sector (table 23), backward caste membership associates with better performance in financing, provisioning, and M&E, and forward caste membership associates with better provisioning and external coordination. The importance of caste in the women's development sector is reinforced by experience in Karnataka highlighted in box 8.

Caste is not particularly significant in the water supply and sanitation sector, although a small pro–scheduled caste bias is apparent in relation to community-based action and information sharing. It is more significant in watershed, but findings—while not favoring scheduled castes—appear to be slightly less skewed in favor of high-caste status in this sector than in the women's sector.

The poverty status of members does not seem to affect organizational performance (annex table A14). The exception is in the watershed sector, in which there is a positive association between capacity building and poverty rank. The landholding status of members also has little significance for performance, with the exception of a positive relationship with capacity building and information sharing in the water supply and sanitation sector (annex table A15).

Table 23 Household Caste/Religious Group and Performance

(See annex table A32)

		Function								
Sector	*Caste/religious group*	*1*	*2*	*3*	*4*	*5*	*6*	*7*	*8*	*9*
Women	Scheduled tribe	+	o	+	o	o	o	o	++	o
	Backward caste	+	o	++	o	o	o	+	o	o
	Forward caste	o	o	++	o	o	++	+	o	o
	Minority	o	o	o	o	o	o	o	o	++
Water/sanitation	Scheduled tribe	o	*	o	—	o	o	o	o	—
	Backward caste	o	*	o	-	o	-	o	o	—
	Forward caste	o	*	o	o	o	-	o	o	-
	Minority	o	*	o	-	o	o	o	o	—
Watershed	Scheduled tribe	o	o	o	o	o	o	+	++	—
	Backward caste	o	o	o	o	o	++	o	o	o
	Forward caste	o	o	+	o	o	++	o	+	o
	Minority	+	o	++	o	++	++	++	+	o

Sources: Household questionnaire.

Functions: 1 = financing; 2 = staffing; 3 = provisioning; 4 = community-based action; 5 = capacity building; 6 = coordination of activities; 7 = M&E; 8 = governance; 9 = information sharing/dissemination.

Note: Scheduled caste is the reference category.
  + Significant positive association at 95 percent.
++ Significant positive association at 99 percent.
  - Significant negative association at 95 percent.
— Significant negative association at 99 percent.
  o No significant association.
  * Insufficient data. Relatively few local organizations undertook activities falling under the general function area of staffing. In the case of the drinking water and sanitation projects, in which this problem was particularly acute, this function has not been included in the analysis.

Attendance at meetings has some significance for the performance of women's sector projects, but even more for rural water supply and sanitation projects. However, in the watershed sector, attendance associates negatively with staffing and positively with information sharing (annex table A16).

External Environment

Five village characteristics are used to assess how the setting of local organizations associates with performance of the nine main functions. Variables

---

Box 8 Caste Differences Complicate
Organizational Performance

In Rajapura in Chitradurga district, a multicaste village with sharp economic divisions, a Stree-Shakthi group was formed with members of different castes. The SC households were agricultural laborers, while the others were landed cultivators, and these subgroups of members developed different expectations of the group. Because the anganawadi worker stayed in a different village, she could not conduct night meetings, and usually conducted them during the day. The wage laborers stated at the beginning that they could not attend meetings during the work day and would expect the staff to collect savings from their doorsteps. Women belonging to the upper castes did attend the daytime meetings. This led to a more intimate relationship between the staff and those members. The SC women, meanwhile, felt that because the anganawadi worker belonged to the upper caste she was biased toward her caste people and was neglecting the SC women. They alleged that the worker had misappropriated the group savings, and the issue had not yet been resolved when the fieldwork was conducted. The anganawadi worker complained that the SC women did not attend any training programs conducted outside the village, while the latter took the position that their livelihood demands were such that they could not afford to lose one day's wage.

The study team found that the anganawadi worker was not able to understand or deal with the problems arising from caste heterogeneity. She took the position that the SC women were illiterate, ignorant, and irresponsible. The study team had a different impression of the SC women, who were raising issues relating to participation, transparency, and accountability. These factors have in fact had an adverse impact on the functioning of the group, which after functioning well between October 2000 and December 2001, was disbanded in February 2002.

Source: Case studies.

---

include distance to market, number of households in a village, the amount of irrigated land in a village, whether or not it is a project village, and the state in which the village is located. Table 24 presents the findings from regression analysis of core characteristics of the villages where the sample organizations are operating.

Distance to market associates negatively with performance of most functions in the women's development sector, but it has positive significance for many functions in the other two sectors.[19] The farther away a village is

Table 24 Village Characteristics and Performance

(See annex table A32)

Sector	Characteristic	1	2	3	4	5	6	7	8	9
		\multicolumn{9}{c}{Function}								
Women	Distance to market	—	-	-	°	—	°	—	—	—
	Number of households	°	++	—	+	°	°	++	°	°
	Irrigated land	°	°	++	+	++	°	++	++	°
	Project village[a]	++	°	°	°	°	++	+	+	°
	Madhya Pradesh	—	-	°	°	—	°	°	°	°
Water/ sanitation	Distance to market	°	*	++	—	++	++	++	+	++
	Number of households	°	*	+	++	++	++	°	++	++
	Irrigated land	—	*	°	°	°	°	°	°	°
	Project village[a]	°	*	°	°	°	°	°	°	°
	Uttaranchal	°	*	°	°	++	++	++	++	++
Watershed	Distance to market	++	°	++	++	++	++	++	++	++
	Number of households	+	++	++	°	++	°	++	++	++
	Irrigated land	—	°	°	°	—	++	°	°	°
	Project village[a]	°	°	°	°	°	°	°	°	°
	Uttaranchal	++	°	°	++	++	++	++	++	++

Sources: Village-level and household questionnaires.

Note: Functions: 1 = financing; 2 = staffing; 3 = provisioning; 4 = community-based action; 5 = capacity building; 6 = coordination of activities; 7 = M&E; 8 = conflict resolution/accountability; 9 = information sharing/dissemination.

a. The variable project village identifies a village that comes under a World Bank–aided intervention (or in the case of watershed development in Karnataka, one aided by the Department for International Development).

 +   Significant positive association at 95 percent.
++   Significant positive association at 99 percent.
 -   Significant negative association at 95 percent.
—   Significant negative association at 99 percent.
 °   No significant association.
 *   Insufficient data. Relatively few local organizations undertook activities falling under the general function area of staffing. In the case of the drinking water and sanitation projects, in which this problem was particularly acute, this function has not been included in the analysis.

from a market, the better the organization performs. In all sectors, the size of a village has a positive relationship with performance, although results in the women's sector were mixed: a larger village population associates positively with staffing, community-based action, and M&E, but negatively with provisioning.

The amount of irrigated land in a village has little association with any function in the water supply and sanitation sector except financing. In watershed, it associates negatively with financing and capacity building, but positively with coordination of activities. In the women's development sector, higher amounts of irrigated land relate to better organizational performance in provisioning, capacity building, M&E, and conflict resolution.

The presence of a World Bank–aided project is only significant in the women's development sector. Finally, in terms of states, local organizations in Uttaranchal perform significantly better than those in Karnataka for the water supply and sanitation and watershed sectors. However, for women's development, the only significant pattern is that organizations in Madhya Pradesh appear to be more able to address conflict and better at sharing information.

Summary

The importance of linkages and context for effective performance of local organizations varies significantly by sector. Findings suggest a need for caution when making assumptions in program design about how these factors will influence outcomes.

While linkages among local organizations are considered useful for strengthening organizations and avoiding duplication in environments with limited resources, there is variation in what types of linkages appear to be important in different sectors. Linkages with elected governments are generally high; linkages with administrative government are low in the women's development and watershed sectors, but high in the water supply and sanitation sector. Linkages with other local organizations are low across sectors, ranging from 29 percent with such linkages in the watershed development sector to 60 percent in the water supply and sanitation sector.

This analysis suggests that it is not just the number of linkages that is important, but the nature of the relationships and the needs of each sector. Relationships with LDs, panchayats, and other organizations associate with successful outcomes in some sectors more than in others. Women's development organizations, for example, actually appear to suffer more than benefit from a relationship with LDs, whereas in the other two sectors there are apparent benefits.

Similarly, the internal composition of organizations has significance particular to each sector. Factors such as social composition and gender of household head were important determinants of quality of organizational performance only in the women's development sector. Factors such as poverty rank or land ownership did not significantly impact performance, except capacity building in the watershed sector, and capacity building and information sharing in the water and sanitation sector.

Regarding the external environment, organizations performed significantly better in both sectors studied in Uttaranchal than in Karnataka (water supply and sanitation and watershed), while women's development organizations in Karnataka showed a tendency to perform better than those in Madhya Pradesh. The distance of a village to market mattered, but again the relationship varied by sector. Proximity was important in the women's development sector and had a negative impact in water supply and sanitation and watershed. Similarly, village size had a negative relationship with performance in the water supply and sanitation and watershed sectors.

The amount of irrigated land in a village had little effect in the water supply and sanitation sector, mixed effects in watershed, and positive influences in the women's development sector. Finally, apart from positive outcomes in a few functions in the women's development sector, organizations operating in a village with a World Bank or DFID-aided intervention did not perform much differently from organizations in villages benefiting from any other form of sector intervention.

Notes

18. This may be explained to an extent by the fact that these agencies have quite specific roles to play according to the project design for projects studied in this sector.

19. Distance to market serves as an indicator of the extent to which a village is interacting with external markets in terms of commodity flows both into and out of the village. It is also indicative of the direction and pace of development as it reflects the degree to which a village is open to the movement of people as laborers, government employees, businessmen, students, and consumers, and the flows of ideas and information that accompany these movements of people in rural India.

VI

Equity, Sustainability, and Organizational Performance

In addition to organizational effectiveness, two other dimensions of organizational performance were investigated: equity in participation and delivery of benefits, and organizational and benefit sustainability. Results for each are described in this section.

Equity

Two aspects of equity outcomes are examined: participation in decision making, and receipt of development benefits.

Equity in Decision Making

Participation in collective decision making is argued to be a necessary condition for equitable and sustainable development outcomes. Such participation is seen to ensure that the interests of marginalized groups are voiced and considered, that all participants accept collective responsibility for the decisions made, and that the subsequent activities undertaken are collectively owned. Collective decision making is expected to lead to better distribution of benefits (greater equity) and to increase people's motivation to engage in the work of local government.

Equity in decision making is measured in two ways. The first is by looking at the organizational positions of the individuals who appoint office-holders and who participate in key decisions. These data give insight into the democratic functioning of an organization. The second is through analysis of the poverty status of decision makers, which helps reveal the extent to which processes and outcomes may or may not be pro-poor.

Annex tables A17, A18, and A20 present reports from household surveys on participation in decision making in the three sectors. Responses indicate that both the position a person holds in an organization and a person's poverty rank affect his or her ability to influence decision making in each sector.

In the women's development sector, organization members are deeply involved in the selection of their representatives and strongly represented

65

in final decisions on key issues such as loan disbursal, repayments, and corrective action (annex table A17). Exploring differences by poverty rank shows that the women's development projects operate in an equitable, but not pro-poor manner. The poverty rank of respondents has little effect on their participation in making important decisions in either state.

In the water supply and sanitation sector, the situation is very different. More than one-third of those interviewed in Karnataka did not know how officeholders were selected (annex table A18). However, those who did know reported that members were the most highly involved of all participants in the selection of officeholders. While influential members did not play a major role in the selection of officeholders, they do have some influence and this is strongest in Uttaranchal. In this sector, poverty in Uttaranchal seems to have a minor impact on a person's influence in making key decisions in an organization (annex table A19). The chances of a middle or wealthy member of an organization making final decisions are only marginally higher than for members in lower poverty ranks. However, in Karnataka wealthier representatives and presidents are more likely to dominate final decisions.

Of even more concern is the finding that in Karnataka three-quarters of members belonging to very poor and poor groups did not know how decisions were made. Wealthier representatives and presidents are more likely to dominate final decisions. Water supply and sanitation organizations in Karnataka are not functioning as the collective management units envisaged in project documentation.

In the watershed sector, levels of knowledge of decision making were high (annex table A20). Respondents indicated that across organizational types and states, members took part in selecting officeholders. However, one-fifth of respondents did not know whether representatives were involved in making key decisions. The watershed sector demonstrates a minor pro-poor bias in terms of decision-making roles (annex table A21). While levels of knowledge of decision making were reasonable, fewer wealthy people than poor people in Uttaranchal knew how decisions were made.

Equity in Delivery of Benefits

Because all of the projects studied purport to be poverty alleviation projects, a key question is who receives the benefits. The nature of benefits to members varies from sector to sector and, to a lesser extent, from project to project.

- In the women's development and empowerment sector the benefits analyzed include (a) the number of loans obtained from the local organization to which a member belonged, (b) the quality of credit delivery from the local organization to which a member belonged, and (c) the quality of credit delivery from banks.

- For rural water supply and sanitation projects the study assessed (a) reduction in time required to collect clean drinking water, (b) improvement in individual sanitary facilities, and (c) availability of new facilities for washing clothes.
- Watershed management benefits are defined as (a) prevention of soil erosion and water loss, and (b) increase in a respondent's household agricultural production.

Women's development interventions achieve the most equity in distribution of benefits among the three sectors studied. Regression results indicate that factors including social grouping, land ownership, and poverty rank do not significantly associate with the number of loans received (annex table A22). Minorities are only slightly more likely than other groups to receive loans.

However, this is not without caveats. Nearly half of all women's SHG members had not yet received a loan from their organization, but 33 percent had received two or more loans. Table 25 shows that, while 18 percent of the very poor have received three or more loans, 48 percent have received no loans at all. This is potentially problematic because the very poor have the greatest need and least capacity to secure credit from the rural banking sector. If they cannot secure credit from a local organization, they will have to pay exorbitant interest rates for loans taken with local moneylenders.

Because of the nature of the good, it is difficult to target only the poor in water supply and sanitation sector interventions. Dissatisfaction with provision of both sanitary and washing facilities was fairly equally distributed across poverty groups. However, the key benefit delivered—access to clean drinking water—shows a bias in favor of wealthier households. Half of households in the lowest two poverty ranks thought there had been no improvement, whereas only one-third of respondents from the top two poverty ranks found this to be the case (table 26). Despite these ratings, regression analysis found no significant association between different poverty

Table 25 Number of Loans Obtained by Poverty Ranking

Poverty ranking	0 loans (%)	1 loan (%)	2 loans (%)	3 loans (%)	4 loans (%)	N
Very poor	48	20	14	12	6	315
Poor	40	28	18	9	5	372
Middle	42	24	17	11	6	256
Wealthy	65	10	13	9	3	107
Average across all ranks (N)	45 (475)	23 (243)	16 (166)	11 (111)	5 (55)	1,050

Source: Household questionnaire.

Table 26 Members' Assessment of Their Local Organization's Performance in Improving Access to Clean Drinking Water, by Poverty Ranking

Poverty ranking	Poor (%)	Adequate (%)	Good (%)	N
Very poor	21	20	59	251
Poor	28	21	51	336
Middle	18	17	65	283
Wealthy	16	18	66	194
Average across all ranks (N)	22 (229)	19 (203)	59 (632)	1,064

Source: Household questionnaire.

status or any other variable (except state, in which living in Uttaranchal has a significant positive association) and improved access to clean drinking water or improved sanitary facilities (annex tables A23 and A24).

In the watershed sector, delivery of benefits appears to disproportionately benefit the wealthy, particularly those with large landholdings. The poor and very poor were more likely to be dissatisfied with performance of local organizations in both preventing soil erosion and water loss, and in improving agricultural production. Conversely, the middle and wealthy were most likely to rate performance in these areas as good (annex tables A25 and A26). When looking at ratings by size of landholdings, satisfaction with performance increases quite clearly with the size of landholding in both areas (annex tables A27 and A28). Regression analysis reinforces this when significant positive associations are found between landholdings of more than one acre and the highest perception of benefits received from soil erosion prevention and agricultural production interventions (annex tables A29 and A30).

Sustainability

Sustainability was investigated in terms of perceived sustainability of benefits delivered by organizations, as well as the potential for the organization itself to remain in existence over time.

Sustainability of Benefits

With nearly three-quarters of all respondents predicting that key benefits would continue in the future, the overall assessment of benefit sustainability by respondents in all three sectors was relatively high (table 27). Figures were best for women's groups, at 90 percent, followed by water supply and sanitation and watershed organizations, both around 70 percent. State

Table 27 Sustainability of Benefits, by Sector

Sector ·	Not sustainable (%)	Sustainable (%)	Missing data (%)	N
Women	10	89	1	1,055
Water/sanitation	29	71	0	1,148
Watershed	30	68	2	1,075
Average across sectors (N)	23 (757)	76 (2,482)	1 (39)	3,278

Source: Household questionnaire.

disparities were apparent in the latter two sectors: more respondents in Karnataka than in Uttaranchal thought benefits were sustainable (28 percent more in watershed and 17 percent more in water and sanitation). In terms of types of organization, project-initiated CBOs were considered more likely to have generated sustainable benefits than other types of CBOs.

Organizational Sustainability

An initial indicator of a local organization's sustainability is the length of time it has been in existence. The expansion of local organizations gained momentum in the late 1990s (annex table A31). Before 1998, only 38 of the 254 CBOs in the studied communities existed. The remainder emerged over the following five-year period. This is unsurprising, as the majority of the sample local organizations were formed more or less as a direct consequence of the development of the interventions studied. In addition, these findings do not support the often-heard accusations that project planners ignore the presence of large numbers of preexisting local organizations when designing new interventions. However, the fact that the majority of sector-related organizations found in villages were project- or government-initiated CBOs suggests a degree of program dependency that could be a problem for future organizational sustainability.

A second indicator of sustainability is the percentage of meetings attended by an organization's members. While an imperfect measure, attendance can reflect the participatory nature of the organization and, to some degree, the sense of commitment possessed by its members. A common assumption in project design is that poor participation and a weak sense of member commitment augurs badly for a local organization's sustainability. While this assumption is not tested here, attendance is reported as an initial yet admittedly inconclusive sign of the potential for organizational sustainability.

The women's development sector enjoys the highest level of attendance, with 95 percent of respondents saying they attend meetings (table 28). Only half of respondents in the water supply and sanitation sector attend meetings, while just over 60 percent attend watershed organization meetings. These

Table 28 Member Attendance of Local Organization Meetings, by Sector

Sector	Never attend (%)	Sometimes attend (%)	Always attend (%)	N
Women	5	20	75	1,039
Water/sanitation	50	32	18	1,147
Watershed	39	31	30	1,058
Average across sectors (N)	31 (1,019)	28 (876)	41 (1,349)	(3,244)

Source: Household questionnaire.

differences are easily explained. The core activities of rural women's development and empowerment groups are savings and credit, and attendance is closely linked to credit allocation. Thus, high levels of participation are critical to the core business of these organizations. However, the same is not true for the other sectors.

A third indicator of sustainability is management of an organization. In particular, the locus of management reflects both the degree of members' commitment to the local organization and the organization's capacity to exist without external support. As table 29 shows, most organizations (64 percent) are seen to be managed by members. Figures range from 53 percent in the women's development interventions to 75 percent in the rural water supply and sanitation projects. Data are also presented according to the local organization types present in each sector. The most interesting point to emerge is that the project-initiated CBOs have a high level of member-based management, significantly higher than government- or NGO-initiated CBOs.

A final indicator of organizational sustainability is the sustainability of financial resources. As indicated in section III, financial assets are currently inadequate. How likely, then, are organizations to generate financial resources independent of project or external support? One way in which they can do this is through contributions from their members. However, table 30 shows that approximately 25 percent of all organizations in women's and watershed development do not receive financial contributions (other than loan repayments) from members, and this figure more than doubles in the drinking water sector. Across sectors, project-initiated CBOs are more likely to receive contributions than any other type of local organization.

With such limited track records of generating their own financial resources, perceptions of financial sustainability tend to depend on whether support from outside organizations is secure and expected to continue. Table 31 shows officials' assessments of the adequacy of their organizations' internally generated financial resources. In illustration, staff from the LDs

Table 29 Local Organizations Managed by the Members, by Local Organization Type and Sector

Local organization type	All			Women			Water/sanitation			Watershed		
	No (%)	Yes (%)	N	No (%)	Yes (%)	N	No (%)	Yes (%)	N	No (%)	Yes (%)	N
NGO	100	0	1	100	0	1	n.a.	n.a.	n.a.	n.a.	n.a.	n.a.
CBO-GI	52	48	62	55	45	53	n.a.	n.a.	n.a.	33	67	9
CBO-NI	58	42	12	64	36	11	n.a.	n.a.	n.a.	0	100	1
CBO-PI	29	71	173	38	62	58	22	78	58	28	72	57
CBO-SI	0	100	2	0	100	2	n.a.	n.a.	n.a.	n.a.	n.a.	n.a.
Average across all organizations	36	64	269	47	53	125	25	75	58	29	71	67

Source: Local organization officials questionnaire.

Note: CBO-GI = community-based organization (government-initiated); CBO-NI = community-based organization (NGO-initiated); CBO-PI = community-based organization (project-initiated); CBO-SI = community-based organization (self-initiated); NGO = nongovernmental organization.
n.a. Not applicable.

Table 30 Local Organizations Receiving Regular Financial Contributions from Members, by Type and Sector

Local organization type	All			Women			Water/sanitation			Watershed		
	No (%)	Yes (%)	N	No (%)	Yes (%)	N	No (%)	Yes (%)	N	No (%)	Yes (%)	N
LD	44	56	18	n.a.	n.a.	n.a.	44	56	18	n.a.	n.a.	n.a.
GP	75	25	32	n.a.	n.a.	n.a.	75	25	32	n.a.	n.a.	n.a.
NGO	0	100	1	0	100	1	n.a.	n.a.	n.a.	n.a.	n.a.	n.a.
CBO-GI	32	68	65	32	68	56	n.a.	n.a.	n.a.	33	67	9
CBO-NI	42	58	12	45	55	11	n.a.	n.a.	n.a.	0	100	1
CBO-PI	35	65	209	23	77	60	50	50	92	25	75	57
CBO-SI	0	100	2	0	100	2	n.a.	n.a.	n.a.	n.a.	n.a.	n.a.
Average across all organizations (N)	39 (132)	61 (207)	339	28 (37)	72 (93)	130	55 (78)	45 (64)	142	25 (17)	75 (50)	67

Source: Local organization officials questionnaire.

Note: CBO-GI = community-based organization (government-initiated); CBO-NI = community-based organization (NGO-initiated); CBO-PI = community-based organization (project-initiated); CBO-SI = community-based organization (self-initiated); GP = gram panchayat; LD = line department.

n.a. Not applicable.

Table 31 Local Organizations' Assessments as to Whether They Have Sufficient Internal Resources, by Local Organization Type and Sector

Local organization type	All			Women			Water/sanitation			Watershed		
	No (%)	Yes (%)	N	No (%)	Yes (%)	N	No (%)	Yes (%)	N	No (%)	Yes (%)	N
LD	0	100	18	n.a.	n.a.	n.a.	0	100	18	n.a.	n.a.	n.a.
GP	56	44	34	n.a.	n.a.	n.a.	56	44	34	n.a.	n.a.	n.a.
NGO	0	100	1	0	100	1	n.a.	n.a.	n.a.	n.a.	n.a.	n.a.
CBO-GI	54	46	65	57	43	56	n.a.	n.a.	n.a.	33	67	9
CBO-NI	50	50	12	55	45	11	n.a.	n.a.	n.a.	0	100	1
CBO-PI	33	67	211	42	58	60	n.a.	n.a.	n.a.	20	80	59
CBO-SI	100	0	2	100	0	2	36	64	92	n.a.	n.a.	n.a.
Average across all organizations (N)	38 (132)	62 (211)	343	50 (65)	50 (65)	130	36 (52)	64 (92)	144	22 (15)	78 (54)	69

Source: Local organization officials questionnaire.

Note: Internal resources include funds generated by the local organization or now owned by the local organization; that is, they could include a capital grant from a donor. CBO-GI = community-based organization (government-initiated); CBO-NI = community-based organization (NGO-initiated); CBO-PI = community-based organization (project-initiated); CBO-SI = community-based organization (self-initiated); GP = gram panchayat; LD = line department.
n.a. Not applicable.

in the water and sanitation sector perceive there to be no problem with their internal resources. This is not surprising because their internal resources are based on departmental budgetary allocations, which in India tend to be quite stable for staff and other recurrent expenditures, and are increased annually on the basis of a ministry's general budget increase.[20] Project-initiated CBOs also record a relatively high degree of financial security; again, their budgets are based on program allocations that are not expected to change within the project's lifetime. These findings are also broadly consistent with those in table 9 above (section III), in which LDs and project-initiated CBOs (at least in the watershed sector) were the only local organizations to report adequate financial asset bases.

Excluding the single NGO, all of the other types of local organizations— none of which have stable sources of financing—are much less positive about their resource position. Assessments are almost equally divided between those who believe their own internal resources are sufficient and those who do not. Less than half of all GPs report adequate internally generated resources.

Summary

Analysis of indicators of equity in participation in decision making and delivery of benefits shows considerable variation across sectors. In decision making, the women's development sector shows broad and largely equitable participation. In the watershed sector, there is also broad participation in decision making, and a slight pro-poor bias in knowledge of decision-making roles. In the water and sanitation sector, however, knowledge of decision-making procedures is low, and wealthier representatives and office-holders appear to have higher levels of influence, particularly in Karnataka.

The women's development sector also demonstrates equity in distribution of benefits. In the other two sectors, however, key benefits appear to disproportionally reach wealthier households. This is particularly strong in the watershed sector, in which regression analysis reinforces reported dissatisfaction with performance of local organizations among the poor.

With nearly three-quarters of all respondents predicting that key benefits would continue in the future, the overall assessment of benefit sustainability by respondents in all three sectors was relatively high. Clear patterns for organizational sustainability are less easily found from the data presented above. In addition, these indicators, particularly for attendance, provide only crude information regarding how well an organization performs and how likely it is to sustain itself. Not all organizations require regular attendance of all members, as executive committees can often handle routine business.

However, when combining these indicators with others considered to associate with sustainability (attendance, participation in decision making, awareness of business rules and organizational activities, self-management, capacity to generate funds), the story becomes more telling. Table 32 provides

Table 32 Summary Figures on Sustainability

(Percent)

	All		Women		Water/sanitation		Watershed	
	Negative	Positive	Negative	Positive	Negative	Positive	Negative	Positive
Meeting Attendance (Table 28, section VI)	31	69	5	95	50	50	39	61
Self-Managed (Table 29, section VI)	36	64	47	53	25	75	29	71
Meeting Minutes Read (Table 13, section IV)	40	60	35	65	58	42	25	75
Meeting Information Passed through Word of Mouth (Table 14, section IV)	77	23	87	13	58	42	87	13
Decisions Made by Consensus (Tables 16 and 17, section IV)	n.a.	n.a.	6	94	46	54	9	91
Representatives' Awareness of Rules (Table 11, section IV)	17	83	23	77	16	84	6	64
Members' Awareness of Rules (Table 12, section IV)	26	74	29	71	23	77	23	77
Regular Financial Contributions from Members (Table 30, section VI)	39	61	28	72	55	45	25	75

Sources: Household and local organization officials questionnaires.

Note: Assessments drawn from existing analysis, "negative"/"positive" values correspond to the following: row 1, never (negative) and sometimes/always (positive); rows 2 and 3, no (negative) and yes (negative) and no (positive); row 4, yes (negative) and sometimes/always (positive); row 5, Don't Know/Not at All (negative) and Potentially/To a Large Extent (positive); row 6, None (negative) and Some/All (positive); rows 7 and 8, no (negative) and yes (positive).

n.a. Not available.

summary indicators of sustainability presented in different sections of this paper.[21]

The women's development and watershed sectors demonstrate the most consistently positive indications of sustainability, with the exception of member participation in management in women's development. Organizations in the water supply and sanitation sector perform quite poorly in most indicators with the exceptions of member management and awareness of rules (representatives and members), in which positive results are highest among the three sectors. Organizations in this sector appear to have the smallest chance of sustaining themselves.

Notes

20. Nonrecurrent expenditures and discretionary funds, however, are often quite limited among administrative government at the local level.

21. The table also notes when a more detailed discussion of each of these is provided in this paper.

VII
Summary of Findings and Their Operational Implications

Local organizations appear set to remain key actors in decentralized rural development activities supported by government and donor agencies in India. The interventions studied here have diversified the organizational landscape in all sectors. LDs are no longer singularly responsible for activities—elected government bodies are mandated roles in sector interventions (albeit often limited in number and type) and the practice of working through village-level CBOs has firmly taken root. These organizations—of whatever provenance or type—are regarded by those sponsoring and designing interventions as improving effectiveness, ensuring that benefits reach those most in need, and enhancing local capacities to articulate, prioritize, and respond to their own needs.

This section first summarizes the core findings of the research and then suggests options for enhancing the effectiveness of the local organizational landscape in decentralized interventions.

Core Findings

Despite broadening the range of local organizational actors in the three sectors studied, *administrative government bodies (LDs) remain, by design, deeply involved down to the village level.* Combined with the limited role allocated to and played by elected governments, this indicates that decentralization in these sectors remains essentially a matter of deconcentration for LDs, rather than a true decentralization in the spirit of the 73rd amendment to the Constitution. In addition—

- Administrative government bodies are placed firmly in control of budgets, policy, and activities, at least through the district and block levels. At the village level, numbers of organizations are far greater and decision making over budgets and activities is no longer purely under their control.
- The role of district-level elected government is limited on paper and in practice; block-level PRIs play no role in any sector; and only in the drinking water and sanitation sector are village-level GPs mandated a substantial role.

The presence of interventions is largely responsible for increasing the number of village-level organizations. Reflecting this, more than 85 percent of all village-level organizations in the study had been established since 1998. Contradicting the popular belief that villages host a high number and wide range of organizations, few were found to be working in the study sectors other than those connected to government or initiated as part of a project. This may not be true for other sectors, but does indicate that much of the concern about creating parallel membership-based organizations or undermining existing organizations is unfounded for these sectors.

The presence of independent NGOs working in the sectors studied was surprisingly low. NGOs were active, but generally as contractors for specific government projects. They reported slightly different working relations with government across sectors and states, but overall they were concerned that their contractual obligations and financial dependence on government placed them in a poor bargaining position. Private sector organizations were noticeably absent from the inventory of organizations studied. This is because they were deemed by respondents to have no role at the village level and no direct role at any other level in any of the sectors. In the women's development sector, banks were expected to be important actors, but the study found that only 14 percent of all village-level SHGs had secured loans from banks.

Frequency of performance of mandated functions varied by state, sector, and type of organization. At the state and district levels, line agencies and project organizations (including support organizations) undertook most of the functions for which they were mandated. At the village level, project-initiated CBOs in the women's development sector undertook 79 percent of mandated functions, but this figure fell to 47 and 46 percent respectively for government- or NGO-initiated CBOs. In the water and sanitation sector, 64 percent of GPs, 61 percent of LDs, and 57 percent of project-initiated CBOs did what they were mandated to do. In the watershed sector, 44 percent of government-initiated CBOs and 70 percent of project-initiated CBOs undertook mandated functions.

Three core findings emerge from data on frequency of functions performed:

- Many functions mandated to local organizations are undertaken—albeit at a lower frequency than envisaged in design. Many organizations also undertake functions for which they have no mandate and there is frequently a transfer of mandated responsibility between organizations.
- Project organizations and project-initiated CBOs perform mandated functions more frequently than other types of local organizations.
- There are state differences in the frequency with which organizations perform functions, but these differences are not as regular or as significant as one might expect given the different policy contexts of the three states.

Undertaking functions without mandate indicates that subsidiarity, avoidance of duplication, or responses to unforeseen needs are occurring. Subsidiarity is most commonly found when CBOs undertake functions mandated to support organizations. Transfer of functions primarily occurs when LDs regularly undertake many functions not mandated to them, especially those mandated to GPs. The fact that GPs are commonly found in situations of subsidiarity and duplication implies that the planned roles for the elected and administrative government bodies in local development, which were envisaged in India's decentralization reforms, have yet to be achieved in practice.

Functions undertaken are not necessarily functions performed well. *Quality in performance of functions varies in relation to the type of activity, the type of organization, and the sector.* In particular, performance was generally adequate in the basic functions of organizational administration and management (financing, staffing, provisioning, M&E, and conflict resolution), but poor in more development-oriented functions (community-based action, capacity building, coordination, and information sharing). Project organizations and project-initiated CBOs not only more frequently performed functions (mandated and nonmandated), but also had the highest-quality performance of all local organizations. GPs generally performed less well than other types of local organizations, particularly in relation to development functions.

Key sector-specific findings include the following:

- *In the women's development sector, in general, interventions have not managed to extend the benefits of collective action beyond savings and credit to other areas of empowerment.* Furthermore, the contracting arrangements for NGOs in projects limit their capacity to operate creatively and responsively.
- *In the drinking water and sanitation sector, the multiplicity of actors and rigid delineation of functions was problematic, as was the number of uncoordinated interventions.* Both resulted in duplication of functions and inefficient use of resources.
- *Organizations in the watershed sector reflect the cross-sector patterns—* basic business functions were performed reasonably well and project-initiated CBOs outperformed all other village-level organizations. GP performance in this sector was poor.

Performance of functions may not be as good as it could be, but *development benefits are reaching beneficiaries.* Again though, there is room for improvement. Nearly half of all members of women's SHGs had not yet received a loan from their organization, but 33 percent of respondents had received two or more loans. A third of respondents felt that loan provision from SHGs was poor and three-quarters thought loan provision from banks was poor. In the water and sanitation sector, nearly one-quarter of household respondents thought that access to clean drinking water had not improved, three-quarters indicated provision of sanitation facilities was poor, and more than half thought there had been no improvement in the provision of washing facilities. Twenty-five percent of watershed project beneficiaries perceived no improvement in soil erosion and water loss, and more than one-third saw no improvement in agricultural productivity.

When looking at issues of equity in delivery of benefits, notable sector findings include the following:

- *Women's development interventions achieve the most equity in distribution of benefits,* but this achievement is not without caveats. While there is generally a good degree of equity in the distribution of loans, scheduled tribes, the landless, and the poorest group members rate SHG performance lower than others and these groups are least likely to receive loans.
- Because of the nature of the good, water and sanitation sector interventions are difficult to target accurately. However, high levels of dissatisfaction with provision of both sanitary and washing facilities were fairly equally distributed across poverty groups. But *the key benefit delivered in the water and sanitation sector—access to clean drinking water—shows a bias in favor of wealthier households.* Half of households in the lowest two poverty ranks thought there had been no improvement, whereas only one-third of respondents from the top two poverty ranks found this to be the case.
- In the watershed sector, social group did not associate with benefits in preventing soil erosion and water loss. However, landless people and marginal and small cultivators had the lowest assessments of performance, and *disaggregation by poverty groups demonstrates that the very poor benefit least in the watershed sector.*

Nearly three-quarters of all respondents receiving benefits predicted that these benefits would continue in the future. Figures were best for women's groups, at 90 percent, followed by water and sanitation and watershed organizations, both around 70 percent. State disparities were apparent in the latter two sectors: more respondents in Karnataka than in Uttaranchal thought benefits were sustainable. In terms of types of organizations, project-initiated CBOs were considered more likely to have generated sustainable benefits than other types of CBOs.

Sustainability of organizational entities remains a real issue in all sectors, and as such it raises questions about sustainability of benefits. Without an organizational mechanism to govern and manage the collective action required to yield benefits, it is unlikely that benefit streams will continue to the extent anticipated by members. An organization's mode of operation is considered to associate with sustainability, and analysis of relevant variables demonstrates considerable divergence by sector, state, and organizational type. Key findings include the following:

- *The majority of organizations in the study were established as interventions were launched, suggesting a degree of program dependency that could be a problem for future organizational sustainability.* Organizational representatives, however, indicated that between 60 and 70 percent of organizations were managed by members, independent of a support organization. Figures for the three sectors vary, however, with 53 percent of organizations in the women's development projects operating independently compared with 75 percent of those in the rural water supply and sanitation projects. CBOs in general had the highest dependency on external management.
- *Attendance of organization meetings varies by sector but is generally low.* More than half of all members of water and sanitation organizations and 40 percent in watershed organizations did not attend meetings. In the women's development sector, attendance was far higher—only 5 percent of members said they never attend meetings.
- *Members have varying levels of awareness of organizational transactions and general business discussed in meetings.* Reading aloud minutes from previous meetings is not universally practiced, and minutes are not always made available. Most organizations rely on word of mouth for transmitting information among members about what happens in an organization's meetings. This highly unreliable mechanism is heavily used by all CBOs and, unless backed by available meeting records, renders organizations vulnerable to mismanagement.
- *Involvement in decision making varies by sector.* In the women's development sector, all organizational members of all poverty ranks and social groups were deeply involved in selection of their representatives and were strongly represented in final decisions on key issues. In the water and sanitation sector, more than one-third of those interviewed in Karnataka did not know how officeholders were selected, but nearly three-quarters of members did know how other key decisions were made in their organization. In the watershed sector, findings indicate that while staff of a support organization may be a key party in decision making, appointment of representatives usually occurs with full knowledge of an organization's general membership.
- *Full awareness of organizational rules is low.* Overall, only half of all CBO representatives were aware of some of an organization's rules and nearly 20 percent had no knowledge at all. Representatives of NGO-initiated CBOs had the highest levels of awareness of organizational rules, and representatives of government-initiated CBOs had the lowest. In the sector in which they operated, just under 10 percent of GP representatives admitted they had no knowledge of the rules governing

its involvement in the sector. The proportion of members unaware of organizational rules was higher. Nearly one-third of members of women's development groups and a quarter of members in the water and sanitation and watershed sectors did not know what organizational rules were.

- *Three-quarters of all organizations generated insufficient internal resources to sustain their operations in the future.* A quarter of all organizations in women's development and watershed and more than half in water and sanitation did not receive regular financial contributions from members. This indicates that initial success in securing mandatory contributions has, at present, little bearing on an organization's capacity to ensure a sustained income base.

Four factors were originally hypothesized as determinants of organizational performance: assets, processes, linkages, and context. *Across sectors, 30 percent of organizations reported inadequate human assets, 60 percent had inadequate material assets, and 70 percent had inadequate financial assets.* Obviously, the poor asset position of organizations is serious, but does it affect performance? In terms of human assets, the picture was inconclusive, except that quality of human assets appears to have greater bearing on organizational performance than quantity of staff. The quantum of material assets available to an organization had little effect on performance in the water and sanitation sector, had a negative association with development functions in the women's development sector, and associated negatively with almost all functions in the watershed sector.

Financial assets had the most significant association with an organization's performance:

- In the water and sanitation sector, in which 40 percent of organizations had sufficient financial assets, these associated positively with all core administrative and management functions.
- In the watershed sector, in which half of all organizations reported adequate endowments, there was a strong positive relationship between financial assets and quality of performance of most functions.
- In the women's development sector, the relationship was least noticeable. The only significant association was a positive one with community-based action, perhaps because so many organizations in the sector (70 percent) are underfinanced.

The association between an organization's processes and its performance are sector- and type-specific, as are the explanations.

- Self-monitoring had little significant association with performance, but *members' awareness of governance rules generally associated with good*

performance in all but the watershed sector. Representatives' awareness
of governance rules positively related to performance in all but the water
and sanitation sector—a sector in which the use of accountability rules
was limited and ineffective.

- Availability and use of minutes, and the form in which information was
  transmitted, associated with performance in different ways in each sector.
  Generally speaking, at the current level of evolution of organizations in
  most sectors, *availability of minutes appears not to be critical.* However,
  as organizations move forward into independent and perhaps more
  sophisticated action, this transparency mechanism will likely become
  increasingly important.
- The only generic lesson for design or implementation to be drawn from
  these findings is that *processes must be tailored to the type of organization and to its core business.*

*In a plural organizational landscape, linkages among organizations are
important for ensuring project effectiveness.* There are multiple organizations operating at the local level, including administrative and elected governments, project organizations, and nonproject organizations. Each of
these often has specific skills and roles to play in ensuring delivery of project benefits. Linkages with administrative government, for example, have
significant positive associations for other organizations with most function areas in the watershed sector. Regarding linkages with other organizations, in the water and sanitation sector there is a positive association
with external coordination and M&E. In the watershed sector, linkages to
other organizations primarily have a negative or negligible impact on
performance.

This analysis suggests that *it is not just the number of linkages that is
important, but the nature of the relationships and the needs of each sector.*
Relationships with LDs, panchayats, and other organizations associate with
successful outcomes in some sectors more than in others. Women's development organizations, for example, appear to suffer more than benefit from
a relationship with LDs, whereas in the other two sectors there are apparent benefits.

*Project-based efforts to facilitate these linkages, however, often fall
short.* Coordination committees or multiagency working groups were featured in each sector with the intention of encouraging linkages among local
organizations, usually as part of project design. Few of them were found
to function as intended, however, other than those at the state level in the
water and sanitation and watershed sectors and at the district level in the
watershed sector. The coordination committees rarely included organizations
other than government LDs or government staff of project units, at least in
practice, and were generally used more for monitoring purposes than for
strategic guidance.

Does the internal environment within which an organization operates affect performance?

- *The poverty rank of members does not associate with organizational performance.* The single exception was in the watershed sector, in which organizations performing best in capacity building had wealthier members.
- *The social composition of groups was only significant in the women's development sector,* in which the presence of the two higher-caste groups (backward and forward) associated with good performance.
- *The amount of land owned by members had little relationship with performance,* except in the water and sanitation sector, in which landlessness associated with poorer performance in capacity building and information sharing.
- *Members' attendance of meetings had only a minimal association with organizational performance in watershed, but it related positively to performance in the other sectors.*

The external environment of an organization has a similarly complex association with performance:

- *The state in which organizations were located was associated with an overall difference in some sectors.* Organizations performed significantly better in Uttaranchal than in Karnataka in both sectors studied in those states (water supply and sanitation and watershed). Women's development organizations in Karnataka showed a tendency to perform better than those in Madhya Pradesh.
- *The distance of a village to market mattered,* but again the relationship varied by sector. In the women's development sector, the farther a village is from markets the worse the performance, whereas in water and sanitation and watershed the situation was reversed.
- Similarly, *the size of the village had a negative relationship with performance in the water and sanitation and watershed sectors.* The smaller the village, the better the overall performance. Results in the women's development sector were mixed: a larger village population associated positively with staffing, community-based action, and M&E, but negatively with provisioning.
- Finally, *whether or not a village received support from a World Bank– or DFID-aided project was insignificant in all but the women's development sector.* In the women's development sector, it associated positively with financing, external coordination, M&E, and conflict resolution.

Core Design Issues

This study provides some new insights into the performance of organizations, and using rigorously collected and analyzed information confirms existing anecdotal and scattered evidence on what organizations do, how they do it, and what attributes associate with their performance. As the main body of the report demonstrates, generic findings are difficult to identify and therein lies an important lesson: *The organizational design of any intervention requires tailoring to the development benefit in question.* This may appear obvious, but the specification of organizational functions in documentation is at present strikingly similar across sectors.

This leads to the second point. It is apparent that, to date, the *organizational and institutional arrangements within interventions have received limited attention during design.* Organizational structures and the attributes that govern their performance are critical to implementation. The importance of this aspect of design has grown in tandem with the increase in the number and diversity of organizational actors. In particular, *the role of GPs is poorly conceived and resourced in most interventions* and insufficient attention has been paid to their capacity to control the behavior of LD staff.

Given the current reality of dependency on local organizations, this study indicates that the shape of the organizational landscape and expectations of what an organization is likely to achieve in the short, medium, and long term need to be better addressed during the design and implementation of interventions. This does not mean detailed specification of implementation arrangements before an intervention. Rather, consideration of a range of design principles that could in turn assist in effective implementation is recommended, including the following:

- Recognizing diversity in functions and being pragmatic in allocation of roles to different types of organizations, including coordination committees, multistakeholder working groups, the private sector, and elected governments;
- Equipping organizations with sufficient financial and high-quality human assets;
- Expecting less of local organizations, whose members are generally interested in short-term outcomes and benefits and judge performance on that basis;
- Allowing flexibility in task allocation, and having monitoring systems that encourage local-level learning and management and at the same time do not tie organizations to deliverables that restrict their capacity to evolve or respond to changing circumstances;
- Embedding in monitoring systems indicators that capture both equity and indirect benefits;

- Ensuring that the final clients play a role in annual performance appraisals of support organizations, including GPs and line agencies;
- Establishing incentive systems in support and village organizations that reflect good performance along a range of variables critical to each sector;
- Developing robust recruitment and selection processes for support organizations;
- Allowing, where appropriate to the task, contracting organizations to play a more creative and strategic role building on and effectively utilizing ongoing experience with villagers;
- Investing more in capacity building and organizational functioning, particularly when long-term presence of village-level organizations is important;
- Focusing capacity building not only on administrative skills but also on skills to help support and village organizations manage a broader development role when appropriate; and
- Establishing appropriate expectations when considering broader development goals, which take time to achieve in light of existing political, economic, and social constraints.

Bibliography

Ahmed, Habib. 1999. "Operating Format of Micro-Finance Schemes, Negative Shocks and Poverty." *Savings and Development* 23 (1): 57–66.

Alsop, Ruth. 2004. "Local Organizations in India: Roles and Relationships." Draft Research Report. World Bank, Washington, DC.

Alsop, Ruth, and Nina Heinsohn. 2005. "Measuring Empowerment in Practice: Structuring Analysis and Framing Indicators." Policy Research Working Paper No. 3510. World Bank, Development Economics Research Group, Washington, DC.

Alsop, Ruth, et al. 2005. "Sector Reports." Institute for Social and Economic Change, Bangalore, India.

Andrews, Matthew, and Anwar Shah. 2002. "Voice and Local Governance in the Developing World: What Is Done, to What Effect, and Why?" World Bank, Washington, DC.

Bahl, W. Roy. 2002. "Implementation Rules for Fiscal Decentralization." In *Development, Poverty and Fiscal Policy: Decentralization of Institutions,* ed. M. Govinda Rao. New Delhi: Oxford.

Baland, J. M., and J. P. Platteau. 1996. *Halting Degradation of Natural Resources: Is There a Role for Rural Communities?* Oxford: Clarendon Press.

Bardhan, Pranab, and Dilip Mookherjee. 1999. "Relative Capture of Local and Central Governments: An Essay in the Political Economy of Decentralization." Center for International and Development Economics Research, Institute for Business and Economic Research, University of California at Berkeley.

Bird, Richard M. 2002. "Intergovernmental Fiscal Relations: Universal Principles, Local Applications." In *Development, Poverty and Fiscal Policy: Decentralization of Institutions,* ed. M. Govinda Rao. New Delhi: Oxford.

Bretton, Albert. 1995. *Competitive Governments.* Cambridge, MA: Cambridge University Press.

Bromley, D. W. 1991. *Environment and Economy: Property Rights and Public Policy.* Cambridge, MA: Blackwell.

Buckley, Graeme. 1996. "Rural and Agricultural Credit in Malawi: A Study of the Malawi Mudzi Fund and the Smallholder Agricultural Credit Administration." In *Finance Against Poverty,* ed. David Hulme and Paul Mosley. London: Routledge.

Clay, Edward, and Bernard Schaffer. 1984. *Room for Manoeuvre: An Exploration of Public Policy in Agricultural and Rural Development.* London: Heinemann.

Cox, Aidan, Steen Folke, Lau Schulpe, and Neil Webster. 2002. *Do the Poor Matter Enough? A Comparative Study of European Aid for Poverty Reduction in India.* New Delhi: Concept.

Dreze, Jean, and Amartya Kumar Sen. 1996. *India: Economic Development and Social Opportunity.* New York: Oxford University Press.

Ghatak, Maitreesh. 1999. "Group Lending, Local Information and Peer Selection." *Journal of Development Economics* 60 (1): 27–50.

Ghatak, Maitreesh, and Timothy W. Guinnane. 1999. "The Economics of Lending with Joint Liability: Theory and Practice." *Journal of Development Economics* 60 (1): 195–228.

GOI (Government of India). 1978. "The Sixth Five-Year Plan." Planning Commission, New Delhi.

———. 1999. "Swarnajayanti Gram Swarozgar Yojana: Guidelines." Ministry of Rural Development, New Delhi.

———. 2002a. "Guidelines for Watershed Development (Revised)." Ministry of Rural Development, Department of Land Resources, New Delhi.

———. 2002b. "Ninth Five-Year Plan, 1997–2002: Thematic Issues and Sectoral Programs." Planning Commission, New Delhi.

GOK (Government of Karnataka). 2001. "Karnataka Administrative Reforms Commission: Final Report." Bangalore.

———. 2002. "Stree-Shakthi." Department of Women and Child Development, Bangalore.

Greene, W. H. 2000. *Econometric Analysis.* Englewood Cliffs, NJ: Prentice-Hall.

Hirway, Indira. 1989. "Panchayati Raj at Crossroads." *Economic and Political Weekly* 24 (29): 1663–67.

Jodha, N. S. 1992. "Common Property Resources: A Missing Dimension of Development Strategies." World Bank Discussion Paper 169. World Bank, Washington, DC.

Johnson, Craig. 2001. "Local Democracy, Democratic Decentralisation and Rural Development: Theories, Challenges and Options for Policy." *Development Policy Review* 19 (4): 521–32.

Johnson, Craig, Priya Deshingkar, and Daniel Start. 2003. "Grounding the State: Devolution and Development in India's Panchayats." Working Paper 226. Overseas Development Institute, London.

Kabeer, Naila. 2003. *Gender Mainstreaming in Poverty Eradication and the Millennium Goals.* London: Commonwealth Secretariat, International Development Research Centre, Canadian International Development Agency.

KAWAD (Karnataka Watershed Development Project). 1995. "ODA-Karnataka Watershed Development Project: Final Draft Report." Vol. 1. Overseas Development Administration, London, and Government of Karnataka, Bangalore.

———. 2001. "Mid-Term Evaluation Report: Karnataka Watershed Development Project." Bangalore.

———. 2002. "Project Guidelines (Up to 10-06-2002)." Bangalore.

Kolavalli, Shashi L., and John Kerr. 2002. "Mainstreaming Participatory Watershed Development." *Economic and Political Weekly* 37 (January 19): 225–42.

Maddala, G. S. 1983. *Limited-Dependent and Qualitative Variables in Econometrics.* New York: Cambridge University Press.

Manor, James. 1995. "Democratic Decentralization in Africa and Asia." *IDS Bulletin* 26 (2): 81–88.

———. 2002. "User Committees: A Potentially Damaging Second Wave of Decentralization." Institute of Development Studies, University of Sussex, Brighton, UK.

McCarten, W. J. 2003. "The Challenge of Fiscal Discipline in the Indian States." In *Fiscal Decentralization and the Challenge of Hard Budget Constraints,* ed. J. Rodden, G. Eskeland, and J. Litvack. Cambridge, MA: MIT Press.

Morduch, Jonathan. 1999. "The Microfinance Promise." *Journal of Economic Literature* 37 (4): 1569–614.

Narayan, Deepa. 1995. "The Contribution of People's Participation: Evidence from 121 Rural Water Supply Projects." Environmentally Sustainable Development, Occasional Paper 1, World Bank, Washington, DC.

North, Douglas. 1990. *Institutions, Institutional Change and Economic Performance.* New York: Cambridge University Press.

Ostrom, Elinor. 1990. *Governing the Commons: The Evolution of Institutions for Collective Action.* New York: Cambridge University Press.

———. 1992. *Crafting Institutions for Self-Governing Irrigation Systems.* San Francisco: Institute for Contemporary Studies Press.

———. 2000. "Collective Action and the Evolution of Social Norms." *Journal of Economic Perspectives* 14 (3): 137–58.

Ostrom, Elinor, Larry Schroeder, and Susan Wynne. 1993. "Analyzing the Performance of Alternative Institutional Arrangements for Sustaining Rural Infrastructure in Developing Countries." *Journal of Public Administration Research and Theory* 3 (1): 11–45.

Parker, Andrew N. 1995. "Decentralization: The Way Forward for Rural Development." Agricultural and Natural Resources Department, World Bank, Washington, DC.

Prud'homme, Rémy. 1995. "The Dangers of Decentralization." *World Bank Research Observer* 10 (2): 201–20.

Rajakutty, S. 1997. "Development of Women and Children in Rural Areas (DWCRA): Are We in the Right Course?" *Journal of Development Studies* 16 (2): 85–112.

Rao, V. M. 2002. "Eradicating Poverty: Some Missing Policy Dimensions." In *Development, Poverty and Fiscal Policy: Decentralization of Institutions,* ed. M. Govinda Rao. New Delhi: Oxford.

Sharma, Manohor, and Manfred Zeller. 1997. "Repayment Performance in Group-Based Credit Programs in Bangladesh: An Empirical Analysis." *World Development* 25 (10): 1731–42.

Stiglitz, J. E. 1990. "Peer Monitoring and Credit Markets." *World Bank Economic Review* 4 (3): 351–66.

Tanzi, Vitto. 1995. "Fiscal Federalism and Decentralization: A Review of Some Efficiency and Macroeconomic Aspects." In *Annual World Bank Conference on Development Economics 1995,* eds. Michael Bruno and Boris Pleskovic. Washington, DC: World Bank.

Uphoff, Norman. 1986. *Local Institutional Development: An Analytical Sourcebook with Cases.* West Hartford, CT: Kumarian Press.

———. 1997. "Institutional Capacity and Decentralization for Rural Development: Technical Consultation on Decentralization." United Nations Food and Agriculture Organization, Rome.

Uphoff, Norman, Milton J. Esman, and Anirudh Krishna. 1998. *Reasons for Success: Learning from Instructive Experiences in Rural Development.* West Hartford, CT: Kumarian Press.

Vedeld, Trond. 2003. "Roles and Relationships in Rural Decentralization: Towards a Multi-Agency Approach." Norwegian Institute for Urban and Regional Research, Oslo.

Walker, David B. 1991. "Decentralization: Recent Trends and Prospects from a Comparative Governmental Perspective." *International Review of Administrative Sciences* 57 (1): 113–29.

Wenner, Mark. 1995. "Group Credit: A Means to Improve Information Transfer and Repayment Performance." *Journal of Development Studies* 32 (2): 263–81.

Westergaard, Kirsten, and Mustafa Alam. 1995. "Local Government in Bangladesh: Past Experiences and Yet Another Try." *World Development* 23 (4): 679–90.

White, Thomas Anderson, and C. Ford Runge. 1995. "The Emergence and Evolution of Collective Action: Lessons from Watershed Management in Haiti." *World Development* 23 (10): 1683–89.

Wooldridge, J. W. 2002. *Econometric Analysis of Cross Section and Panel Data.* Cambridge, MA: MIT Press.

World Bank. 1993. "Karnataka Rural Water Supply and Environmental Sanitation Project: Project Appraisal Report." Washington, DC.

———. 1997. "Staff Appraisal Report on Rural Women Development and Empowerment Project." Report No. 16031-IN, South Asia Country Department II.

———. 1999. "Project Appraisal Document for the Integrated Watershed Development Project (Hills-II)." Rural Development Sector Unit, South Asia Regional Office.

———. 2000. *Overview of Rural Decentralisation in India.* Volume II. New Delhi: World Bank.

———. 2001. "Second Karnataka Rural Water Supply and Sanitation Project." Washington, DC.

———. 2002. *World Development Report 2002: Building Institutions for Markets.* New York: Oxford University Press.

———. 2004. *India Fiscal Decentralization to Rural Governments.* Report No. 26654-IN. Rural Development Sector Unit, South Asia Region, Washington, DC.

Annex

Table A1 Typology of Local Organizations

General category	Organizational type by level
Government	Government administrative (line department)—state level Government administrative (line department)—district level Government administrative (line department)—subdistrict/block level Government administrative (line department)—village level Government administrative (panchayat raj department)—state level Government elected—district level (zilla panchayat) Government elected—subdistrict level (block/taluk panchayat) Government elected—village level (gram panchayat)
Project	Project unit—state level Project unit—district level Project unit—subdistrict level Project unit—village level
Private	NGO for-profit—state level NGO for-profit—district level NGO for-profit—subdistrict level NGO for-profit—village level NGO nonprofit—state level NGO nonprofit—district level NGO nonprofit—subdistrict level NGO nonprofit—village level For-profit—subdistrict level For-profit—village level
Community-based	Community-based organization—government-initiated (village level) Community-based organization—NGO-initiated (village level) Community-based organization—project-initiated (village level) Community-based organization—self-initiated (village level)

Source: Alsop 2004.

Note: NGO = nongovernmental organization.

Table A2 Functions and Subfunctions of Local Organizations

1. Financing

Obtaining funds for the establishment of the study local organization

Provision of funds for the establishment of other local organizations

Obtaining funds for the local organization to facilitate its operation (such as funds to procure seeds, fertilizers, medicines, and so on)

Provision of funds to other local organizations to facilitate their operations

Obtaining funds for the provision and maintenance of physical facilities for members of the sample local organization.

Financial assistance to vulnerable groups such as women, scheduled tribes, and scheduled castes in the sample local organization.

Financial assistance to other local organizations in terms of loans, grants, matching funds, and so on

2. Staffing

Obtaining salaried staff for the sample local organization

Provision of salaried staff for other local organizations

Obtaining staff on deputation from gram panchayat/line department for the local organization

Provision of staff to the other local organizations

3. Provisioning

Obtaining material assets for development works (such as pipes for drinking water schemes)

Provision of material assets for development works of other local organizations

Obtaining community resources or assets (such as land, village water sources) for the temporary or permanent use of the local organization

Provision of community resources or assets (such as land, village water sources) for the temporary or permanent use of the local organization

Provision of services (such as renting out sprayers for profit, and so on)

4. Community-based action

Facilitating periodic repair and maintenance of physical assets for the sample local organization

Mobilizing community involvement for implementing development works of the sample local organization

5. Capacity building

Providing training opportunities for members/beneficiaries of the sample local organization

Enhancing capacity of the local organization to access services from government and other agencies in the district

Table A2 (*continued*)

Ensuring and facilitating incorporation of weaker constituencies (women, scheduled tribes, scheduled castes, and so on) in the activities of the local organization

Providing opportunities to members/beneficiaries to participate in local development programs and activities

Enhancing the capacity of collaborating local organizations to access services and benefits available for members/beneficiaries

6. *Coordination of activities*
Facilitating the establishment of relationships with other local organizations/supporting organizations

Facilitating the access of the sample local organization to external resources (material and financial)

Facilitating the coordination of local organizations among relevant sectors (for example, coordinating the activities of village-level community-based organizations with the local units of line department)

7. *Monitoring and evaluation*
Monitoring activities

Supervising activities

Evaluating performance of works undertaken for local development

Providing guidance to improve effectiveness and minimize shortcomings in the implementation of local development works

8. *Conflict resolution and accountability*
Ensuring the accountability of the members/representatives of the local organization

Ensuring the financial accountability of the local organization

Ensuring representation of vulnerable social groups in the local organization

Providing feedback to gram panchayat/line department/project implementing agency/NGO

Resolving disputes among the various stakeholders

Ensuring that there is accountability in the other local organizations

9. *Information sharing and dissemination*
Sharing the relevant available information with other local organizations

Facilitating the sharing of information among relevant local organizations operating at that level

Sharing information among members (such as personal hygiene in the rural water and sanitation sector)

Source: Alsop 2004.

Note: NGO = nongovernmental organization.

Table A3 Sectors and Projects Selected for the Study

Sector	Projects	Types of local organizations at village level	States in the study
Women's development and empowerment	Swa-Shakthi (Rural Women Development and Empowerment Program)	Self-help groups	Madhya Pradesh Karnataka
	Stree-Shakthi		
	Swarnajayanti Gram Swarozgar Yojna		
Drinking water supply and sanitation	Accelerated Rural Water Supply Program	Village water supply and sanitation committees	Uttaranchal Karnataka
	Integrated Rural Water and Environmental Sanitation	Gram panchayats	
	Swajal		
Watershed development	National Watershed Development Project for Rainfed Areas	Watershed associations	Karnataka Uttaranchal
	Drought Prone Area Program	Micro watershed development committees	
	Desert Development Program	Village development committees	
	Integrated Watershed Development Program—Hills (II)	Gram Resource Management Associations	
	Karnataka Watershed Development (KAWAD) Project	Self-help groups	
	Joint Forest Management Program	User groups	
		Joint forest management committees	

Source: Alsop 2004.

Table A4 Village-Level Instruments

Instrument	Purpose	Respondents
Village-level questionnaire	Build a profile of the village	Data collected from villagers and officials at the village level through a combination of methods (secondary data, poverty ranking, timelines, focus group discussion, organizational mapping)
GP profile	Build a profile of the GP in terms of its human, material, and financial assets and its links with other local organizations	The president or secretary of the GP
Local organization/ SO questionnaires	Build a profile of the local organizations/SOs (other than the GP) operating in the village	The chief of the local organization/SO or any other knowledgeable member of the organization
GP-elected functionaries questionnaire	Learn respondent's assessment of roles, assets, and processes of the GP and its links with other local organizations	The president or vice president of the GP at the time of the survey
Local organization officials questionnaire	Learn respondent's assessment of the sample local organization (including those formed by NGOs, project implementing agencies, and LDs, including self-initiated)	Local organization officeholders
Village-level staff of support organization (LD/NGO/GP) questionnaire	Learn staff assessment of (a) the LD/NGO role in supporting a local organization, and (b) performance of the local organization receiving support	Staff of local organization promoted by LD, NGO, or other organization
Household questionnaire (three versions, adapted to specific sectors)	Gain information on (a) performance and attributes of organization to which household belongs, (b) SO performance, and (c) GP performance	Sample of members of village-level organizations

Source: Alsop 2004.

Note: GP = gram panchayat; LD = line department; NGO = nongovernmental organization; SO = support organization.

Table A5 Number of Organizations Covered in the Study

General category	Organizational type by level	Women[a]	Water/sanitation[b]	Watershed[b]
Government	Government administrative (LD)—state level	2	4	6
	Government administrative (LD)—district level	10	4	15
	Government administrative (LD)—subdistrict/block level	18	6	14
	Government administrative (LD)—village level	51	36	13
	Government administrative (panchayat raj department)—state level	2	2	1
	Government elected—district level (zilla panchayat)	4	4	5
	Government elected—subdistrict level (block panchayat)	12	6	6
	Government elected—village level (gram panchayat)	55	70	42
Project	WB/DFID-initiated project unit—state level	2	2	2
	WB/DFID-initiated project unit—district level	4	6	3
	WB/DFID-initiated project unit—subdistrict level	12	9	10
	WB/DFID-initiated project unit—village level	0	0	0
Private	NGO for-profit—state level	0	0	0
	NGO for-profit—district level	0	0	0
	NGO for-profit—subdistrict level	0	0	0
	NGO for-profit—village level	0	0	0
	Individual for-profit—subdistrict level	0	0	0
	Individual for-profit—village level	0	0	0

Collective action			
NGO nonprofit—state level[c]	0	0	0
NGO nonprofit—district level[c]	0	0	0
NGO nonprofit—subdistrict level[c]	1	0	0
NGO nonprofit—village level[c]	0	0	0
CBO—government-initiated (village level)	51	76	16
CBO—NGO-initiated (village level)	16	0	2
CBO—project-initiated (village level)	60	60	60
CBO—self-initiated (village level)	4	0	0

Source: Alsop 2004.

Note: CBO = community-based organization; DFID = Department for International Development; LD = line department; NGO = nongovernmental organization; WB = World Bank.

a. Summary figures for Karnataka and Madhya Pradesh. Banks were present at the district and taluk levels but were not included in the survey because of their limited function in the sector. Taluk panchayats were reported to play no role in this sector but were included in surveys because of interest in related activities, such as inclusion of marginalized groups in broader development activities.

b. Summary figures for Karnataka and Uttaranchal. Taluk panchayats had no role in this sector but representatives were interviewed.

c. The organizational typology specifies that NGOs functioning as project agencies are classified as project organizations. NGOs are independent of project management in the sectors studied.

Table A6 Functions Undertaken by Village-Level Local Organizations, Drinking Water Supply and Sanitation Sector

(Percentage of local organizations of each type)

Local organization type	N	Financing	Staffing	Provisioning	Community-based action	Capacity building	Coordination	M&E	Conflict resolution	Information
LD	46	9[b]	0[c]	91[b]	30[b]	30[c]	48[c]	26[c]	78[c]	67[c]
GP	21	5[b]	10[b]	100[c]	57[b]	62[c]	86[c]	57[c]	86[b]	62[c]
CBO-PI	56	36[b]	7[b]	89[b]	48[b]	64[a]	64[b]	63[b]	70[b]	82[b]

Source: Local organization officials questionnaire, Drinking Water Supply and Sanitation Sector.

Note: CBO-PI = community-based organization (project-initiated); GP = gram panchayat; LD = line department; SO = support organization.

a. The local organization does not have a mandate to undertake activities in this function area, but the SO that initiated it does.

b. Mandated function for the local organization.

c. Not mandated to the local organization or to its initiating SO.

98

Table A7 Functions Undertaken by Gram Panchayats, Women's Development and Empowerment Sector

Percentage responses from households under differently managed interventions

Function	Karnataka			Madhya Pradesh		
	Swa-Shakthi (N = 257)	*Stree-Shakthi* (N = 220)	*Others* (N = 75)	*Swa-Shakthi* (N = 290)	*SGSY* (N = 155)	*Others* (N = 58)
Resolving conflicts within the local organization	4.3	0.5	0.0	14.5	18.7	39.7
Help in mobilizing benefits from the government and banks for the members	3.1	0.9	0.0	15.9	14.2	15.5
Providing financial assistance (pension to widows, agricultural laborers, support toward housing, loans, and so on) to vulnerable groups	19.8	10.9	24.0	15.5	16.1	15.5
Sending the staff of GP to help the local organization in performing its functions	0.8	0.5	0.0	6.6	4.5	22.4
Instructing the LD staff to provide technical support for the members	4.3	1.4	0.0	11.7	11.6	19.0
Providing the GP building for conducting local organization meetings	10.1	2.7	0.0	14.8	16.8	34.5
Providing village tanks, grazing lands, trees, and so on for collective income-generating activities	3.5	0.9	0.0	7.6	13.5	3.4
Providing opportunities to the local organization members to undertake income-generating activities successfully	2.3	0.9	0.0	13.1	18.1	24.1

(Table continues on the following page.)

99

Table A7 (*continued*)

| | Percentage responses from households under differently managed interventions | | | | | |
| | Karnataka | | | Madhya Pradesh | | |
Function	*Swa-Shakthi* (N = 257)	*Stree-Shakthi* (N = 220)	*Others* (N = 75)	*Swa-Shakthi* (N = 290)	*SGSY* (N = 155)	*Others* (N = 58)
Providing community assets (roads, child care center, and so on) to the local organization members	15.6	5.5	18.7	6.9	12.3	10.3
Facilitating the provision of training to the local organization members	3.1	0.9	0.0	7.9	14.8	10.3
Coordination with LDs in getting benefits to the local organization members	4.7	5.9	0.0	6.6	9.7	8.6
Coordination with other local organizations in resource convergence for the local organization members	1.6	0.5	0.0	5.5	8.4	12.1
Monitoring the local organization activities	2.7	0.5	0.0	6.2	12.3	3.4
Ensuring that the local organization is accountable to members	3.9	0.9	0.0	8.6	18.1	22.4
Ensuring that the local organization incorporates the interests of the poor and vulnerable	7.0	7.3	18.7	8.6	11.6	22.4
Sharing information on GP programs with the local organization members	11.7	5.5	0.0	16.6	15.5	15.5

Source: Household questionnaire.

Note: GP = gram panchayat; LD = line department; SGSY = Swarnajayanti Gram Swarozgar Yojna.

Table A8 Functions Undertaken by Gram Panchayats, Drinking Water Supply and Sanitation Sector

	Percentage responses from households under differently managed interventions					
	Karnataka			Uttaranchal		
Function	IRWES (N = 240)	Line department (N = 216)	Gram panchayat (N = 120)	Swajal (N = 437)	Jal Sansthan (N = 135)	
Providing community assets (roads, child care center, and so on) to the local organization members	63.8	19.4	71.7	18.5	6.7	
Monitoring the local organization activities	59.6	11.1	68.3	23.6	8.1	
Resolving conflicts within the local organization	47.9	12.5	75.0	4.6	3.0	
Help in mobilizing benefits from the government for the members	24.2	7.9	15.0	17.8	29.6	
Providing financial assistance (pension to widows, agricultural laborers, support toward housing, loans, and so on) to the vulnerable groups	36.7	12.0	74.2	79.9	80.0	
Sending staff of GP to help the local organization in performing its functions	58.8	84.7	69.2	14.6	17.0	
Instructing LD staff to provide technical support (water supply, health, and so on) for the members	35.4	10.6	30.0	3.0	17.0	
Providing GP building for conducting local organization meetings	54.6	79.6	63.3	29.5	14.1	
Providing village tanks, grazing lands, trees, and so on for collective income-generating activities	2.9	8.8	50.8	7.1	9.6	

(Table continues on the following page.)

Table A8 (continued)

Function	Percentage responses from households under differently managed interventions				
	Karnataka			Uttaranchal	
	IRWES (N = 240)	Line department (N = 216)	Gram panchayat (N = 120)	Swajal (N = 437)	Jal Sansthan (N = 135)
Providing opportunities to the local organization members in undertaking income-generating activities successfully	0.8	0.0	25.8	13.3	4.4
Facilitating the provision of training (health education and awareness) to the local organization members	7.9	0.0	1.7	8.7	3.7
Coordination with LDs in getting benefits (water quality testing, health support, and so on) to the local organization members	29.2	78.2	65.0	6.4	4.4
Coordination with other local organizations (CBOs, NGOs, and so on) in resource convergence for the local organization members	16.3	4.2	22.5	7.8	4.4
Ensuring that the local organization is accountable to the members	25.4	6.9	56.7	21.7	4.4
Ensuring that the local organization incorporates the interests of the poor and vulnerable	15.4	2.3	60.8	34.3	4.4
Sharing the information on GP programs with the local organization members	53.3	16.7	74.2	41.6	8.9

Source: Household questionnaire.

Note: CBO = community-based organization; GP = gram panchayat; IRWES = Integrated Rural Water and Environment Sanitation Program; LD = line department; NGO = nongovernmental organization.

Table A9 Performance of Functions by Support Organizations, Drinking Water Supply and Sanitation Sector

Percentage responses from households under differently managed interventions citing good performance

Function	IRWES (N = 240)	Karnataka			Uttaranchal		
		Line department (N = 216)	Gram panchayat (N = 120)	Average	Svajal (N = 437)	Jal Sansthan (N = 135)	Average
Administration and Management							
Formation of the local organization	86.3	12.0	19.2	39.2	92.7	14.1	53.4
Explaining how to manage the group	52.5	4.6	13.3	23.5	80.8	11.1	46.0
Monitoring the local organization activities	45.0	29.6	36.7	37.1	65.7	5.9	35.8
Organizing training programs and exposure visits	12.1	1.4	9.2	7.6	76.9	11.1	44.0
Explaining how to improve the habit of making contributions to the local organization	34.6	5.6	5.0	15	67.3	9.6	38.5
Providing capable staff	41.3	24.1	32.5	32.6	62.7	5.2	34.0
Resolving conflicts within the group	30.4	25.0	30.0	28.5	45.5	3.7	24.6
Ensuring that the local organization is accountable to members	18.8	10.2	24.2	17.7	63.8	5.9	34.9
Providing books for accounts maintenance	19.2	6.9	8.3	11.5	70.5	7.4	39.0

(Table continues on the following page.)

Table A9 (*continued*)

Function	*Percentage responses from households under differently managed interventions citing good performance*						
	Karnataka				*Uttaranchal*		
	IRWES (N = 240)	*Line department* (N = 216)	*Gram panchayat* (N = 120)	*Average*	*Swajal* (N = 437)	*Jal Sansthan* (N = 135)	*Average*
Development Oriented							
Training on securing benefits for members	38.3	32.9	12.5	27.9	67.0	6.7	36.9
Coordination with PIA/LD/NGO	47.1	17.1	5.0	23.1	43.7	5.2	24.5
Training on selecting the right technology (borewell, piped water supply, gravity and lift schemes) and making them successful	8.3	0.9	1.7	3.6	62.7	8.9	35.8
Training on how to establish links with GP and LD	26.3	15.7	10.8	17.6	36.8	5.9	21.4
Organizing meetings with government departments to obtain assistance	3.8	1.9	5.0	3.6	36.4	3.0	19.7
Sharing information on waterborne diseases and environmental sanitation	6.3	2.8	2.5	3.9	76.2	6.7	41.5
Sharing information on government programs with the people	45.0	44.4	39.2	42.9	65.4	3.7	34.6

Source: Household questionnaire.

Note: GP = gram panchayat; IRWES = Integrated Rural Water and Environment Sanitation Program; LD = line department; NGO = nongovernmental organization; PIA = project implementation agency.

Table A10 Performance of Functions by Support Organizations, Watershed Development Sector

		Karnataka			Uttaranchal		
				Percentage responses from households under differently managed interventions citing good performance			
Function	KAWAD (N = 455)	Line department and JFMC (N = 112)	Average	GAREMA (N = 430)	Line department and JFM/Van Panchayat (N = 124)	Average
Administration and Management						
Formation of the local organization	97.8	98.2	97.5	97.2	100.0	98.6
Explaining how to manage the group	89.5	75.9	82.7	93.0	100.0	96.5
Providing matching grant to the SHGs	72.5	30.4	51.5	82.1	54.0	68.1
Providing capable staff	91.4	66.1	78.8	82.3	80.6	81.5
Providing books for accounts maintenance	93.6	75.9	84.8	72.6	41.1	56.9
Monitoring the local organization activities	89.0	75.0	82	82.8	74.2	78.5
Resolving conflicts within the group	77.1	47.3	62.2	41.6	3.2	22.4
Ensuring that the local organization is accountable to the members	60.2	39.3	49.8	74.4	55.6	65
Development Oriented						
Coordination with PIA/LD/NGO	78.7	55.4	67.1	44.7	73.4	59.1
Training on how to secure benefits for the members	61.1	40.2	50.7	80.0	58.9	69.5
Organizing training programs and exposure visits	60.4	39.3	49.9	88.4	61.3	74.9

(Table continues on the following page.)

105

Table A10 (*continued*)

| Function | *Percentage responses from households under differently managed interventions citing good performance* | | | | | |
| | *Karnataka* | | | *Uttaranchal* | | |
	KAWAD (N = 455)	*Line department and JFMC* (N = 112)	*Average*	*GAREMA* (N = 430)	*Line department and JFM/Van Panchayat* (N = 124)	*Average*
Explaining how to improve the habit of making contributions to the local organization	73.0	45.5	59.3	78.8	69.4	74.1
Organizing meetings with the government departments to obtain assistance for the members	58.2	34.8	46.5	49.5	42.7	46.1
Training on how to select the right technology, species, and income-generating activities, and how to make them successful	42.9	31.3	37.1	74.7	58.9	66.8
Training on how to establish links with the GP and LD	16.7	9.8	13.3	48.6	32.3	40.5
Sharing information on government programs with the people	51.9	26.8	39.4	72.1	81.5	76.8

Source: Household questionnaire.

Note: GP = gram panchayat; GAREMA = Gram Resources Management Association; JFM = joint forest management; JFMC = Joint Forest Management Committee; KAWAD = Karnataka Watershed Development Project; LD = line department; NGO = nongovernmental organization; PIA = project implementation agency; SHG = self-help group.

Table A11 Performance of Functions by Gram Panchayats, Drinking Water Supply and Sanitation Sector

| | | | | | Percentage responses from households under differently managed interventions citing good performance | | |
| | Karnataka | | | Uttaranchal | | |
Function	IRWES (N = 240)	Line department (N = 216)	Gram panchayat (N = 120)	Swajal (N = 437)	Jal Sansthan (N = 135)
Administration and Management					
Providing community assets (roads, child care center, and so on) to the local organization members	45.4	16.7	55.8	14.0	5.9
Monitoring the local organization activities	48.3	8.3	65.0	19.5	7.4
Resolving conflicts within the local organization	42.5	10.6	55.8	4.6	3.0
Ensuring that the local organization is accountable to the members	16.3	2.3	56.7	20.1	3.7
Sending staff of GP to help the local organization perform its functions	48.3	12.5	67.5	13.7	11.9
Instructing LD staff to provide technical support (water supply, health, and so on) for the members	25.8	8.8	20.0	1.8	7.4
Providing GP building for conducting local organization meetings	45.8	9.3	62.5	25.4	8.9
Providing village tanks, grazing lands, trees, and so on for collective income-generating activities	2.5	8.3	50.8	5.5	7.4

(Table continues on the following page.)

107

Table A11 (continued)

| | Percentage responses from households under differently managed interventions citing good performance | | | | |
| | Karnataka | | | Uttaranchal | |
Function	IRWES (N = 240)	Line department (N = 216)	Gram panchayat (N = 120)	Swajal (N = 437)	Jal Sansthan (N = 135)
Development Oriented					
Coordination with LDs in extending benefits (water quality testing, health support, and so on) to the local organization members	17.9	10.2	61.7	5.3	2.2
Coordination with other local organizations (CBOs, NGOs, and so on) in resource convergence for the local organization members	9.6	4.2	8.3	6.9	4.4
Ensuring that the local organization incorporates the interests of the poor and vulnerable	11.7	2.3	53.3	33.6	3.7
Providing opportunities to the local organization members in undertaking income-generating activities successfully	0.4	0.0	0.8	12.4	2.2
Facilitating the provision of training (health education and awareness) to the local organization members	7.5	0.0	1.7	7.3	1.5
Sharing information on GP programs with local organization members	40.8	7.9	63.3	39.1	8.1
Help in mobilizing benefits from the government for the members	13.8	3.2	5.0	14.9	26.7

Source: Household questionnaire.

Note: CBO = community-based organization; GP = gram panchayat; IRWES = Integrated Rural Water and Environment Sanitation Program; LD = line department; NGO = nongovernmental organization.

Table A12 Performance of Functions by Gram Panchayats, Watershed Development Sector

| | Percentage responses from households under differently managed interventions citing good performance | | | |
| | Karnataka | | Uttaranchal | |
Function	KAWAD (N = 455)	Line department and JFMC (N = 112)	GAREMA (N = 430)	Line department and JFM/Van Panchayat (N = 124)
Administration and Management				
Monitoring the local organization activities	0.0	0.9	35.3	35.5
Resolving conflicts within the local organization	2.9	0.0	3.7	12.9
Ensuring that the local organization is accountable to the members	0.0	0.0	24.0	13.7
Sending the staff of GP to help the local organization in performing its functions	0.0	0.0	18.6	33.9
Instructing the LD staff to provide technical support (such as extension services) for the members	0.7	4.5	19.8	25.8
Providing the GP building for conducting local organization meetings	0.0	0.9	7.9	7.3
Providing village tanks, grazing lands, trees, and so on for collective income-generating activities	3.3	8.0	7.4	30.6
Providing community assets (roads, child care center, and so on) to the local organization members	16.0	7.1	15.1	59.7

(Table continues on the following page.)

Table A12 (*continued*)

| | Percentage responses from households under differently managed interventions citing good performance | | | |
| | Karnataka | | Uttaranchal | |
Function	*KAWAD (N = 455)*	*Line department and JFMC (N = 112)*	*GAREMA (N = 430)*	*Line department and JFM/Van Panchayat (N = 124)*
Development Oriented				
Coordination with the LDs (seeds, saplings, and so on) in getting the benefits to the local organization members	0.2	0.0	24.4	37.1
Coordination with other local organizations in resource convergence for the local organization members	0.7	0.0	17.7	12.1
Help in mobilizing benefits from the government (funds and so on) and banks for the members	1.8	0.9	17.4	18.5
Ensuring that the local organization incorporates the interests of the poor and vulnerable	3.3	0.0	35.8	19.4
Providing opportunities to the local organization members to undertake income-generating activities successfully	0.2	2.7	17.7	21.0
Facilitating the provision of training from agriculture and horticulture departments to the local organization members	0.2	0.0	17.4	6.5
Sharing information on GP programs with the local organization members	5.7	0.0	52.3	56.5

Source: Household questionnaire.

Note: GP = gram panchayat; GAREMA = Gram Resources Management Association; JFM = joint forest management; JFMC = Joint Forest Management Committee; KAWAD = Karnataka Watershed Development Project; LD = line department.

Table A13 Participation in Decision Making by Organizational Position, Drinking Water Supply and Sanitation Sector

(Percent)

	Karnataka					Uttaranchal				
	Do not know	Not at all	Partially	To a large extent	N	Do not know	Not at all	Partially	To a large extent	N
Who appoints officeholders										
Members	32	12	6	50	404	13	24	3	60	570
Influential members	36	46	15	3	403	12	59	26	3	570
Influential nonmembers	38	59	3	0	402	11	82	76	0	568
Locals who initiate the										
organization become leaders	39	54	6	1	394	13	85	2	0	569
The NGO/SO staff	33	57	8	2	397	12	40	35	13	568
GP	33	33	18	16	402	12	78	9	1	568
Who participates in key decisions										
Representatives of local										
organization	25	48	20	7	568	9	34	34	23	557
All members	23	39	14	24	565	0	17	10	73	548
Dominant members	25	62	8	5	562	10	74	14	2	550
GP president	26	26	30	18	576	11	82	6	1	549
GP dominant members	26	44	20	9	565	10	86	4	0	548
Rural elites	26	54	12	8	574	10	74	14	3	546
NGO/SO staff	30	65	4	2	568	8	39	30	23	544

Source: Household questionnaire.

Note: GP = gram panchayat; NGO = nongovernmental organization; SO = support organization.

111

Table A14 Poverty Ranking and Performance

(See annex table A32)

Sector	Poverty rank	1	2	3	4	5	6	7	8	9
		Function								
Women	Poor	o	o	o	-	o	o	o	o	o
	Middle	o	o	o	o	o	o	o	o	o
	Wealthy	-	-	o	o	o	o	o	o	o
Water/	Poor	o	*	o	o	-	o	-	o	o
sanitation	Middle	o	*	o	o	o	o	o	o	o
	Wealthy	o	*	o	o	-	o	o	o	o
Watershed	Poor	o	o	o	o	o	o	o	o	o
	Middle	o	o	o	o	+	o	o	o	o
	Wealthy	o	o	o	o	+	o	o	o	o

Source: Household questionnaire.

Functions: 1 = financing; 2 = staffing; 3 = provisioning; 4 = community-based action; 5 = capacity building; 6 = coordination of activities; 7 = M&E; 8 = governance; 9 = information sharing/dissemination.

Note: Very poor is the reference category.
  + Significant positive association at 95 percent.
  ++ Significant positive association at 99 percent.
  - Significant negative association at 95 percent.
  — Significant negative association at 99 percent.
  o No significant association.
  * Insufficient data. Relatively few local organizations undertook activities falling under the general function area of staffing. In the case of the drinking water and sanitation projects, in which this problem was particularly acute, this function has not been included in the analysis.

Table A15 Household Landholdings and Performance

(See table A32)

Sector	Operational holding	Function								
		1	2	3	4	5	6	7	8	9
Women	0 to 1 acre	o	o	o	o	o	o	o	o	o
	1 to 2.5 acres	o	o	o	o	o	o	o	o	o
	2.5 to 5 acres	o	o	o	o	o	o	o	o	o
	5 to 10 acres	o	o	o	o	o	o	o	o	o
	10+ acres	o	o	o	o	o	o	o	o	o
Water/ sanitation	0 to 1 acre	o	*	o	o	+	o	o	o	++
	1 to 2.5 acres	o	*	o	o	+	o	o	o	++
	2.5 to 5 acres	o	*	o	o	o	o	o	+	++
	5 to 10 acres	o	*	o	o	o	o	o	o	o
	10+ acres	o	*	o	o	+	o	o	o	+
Watershed	0 to 1 acre	o	o	o	o	o	o	+	—	o
	1 to 2.5 acres	o	o	o	o	o	o	o	o	o
	2.5 to 5 acres	o	o	o	o	o	o	o	o	o
	5 to 10 acres	o	o	o	o	o	o	o	o	o
	10+ acres	o	o	o	o	o	o	o	o	o

Source: Household questionnaire.

Functions: 1 = financing; 2 = staffing; 3 = provisioning; 4 = community-based action; 5 = capacity building; 6 = coordination of activities; 7 = M&E; 8 = governance; 9 = information sharing/dissemination.

Note: No cultivation is the reference category.
  + Significant positive association at 95 percent.
  ++ Significant positive association at 99 percent.
  - Significant negative association at 95 percent.
  — Significant negative association at 99 percent.
  o No significant association.
  * Insufficient data. Relatively few local organizations undertook activities falling under the general function area of staffing. In the case of the drinking water and sanitation projects, in which this problem was particularly acute, this function has not been included in the analysis.

Table A16 Gender, Attendance, and Performance

(See table A32)

		Function								
Sector	Characteristic	1	2	3	4	5	6	7	8	9
Women	Woman-headed household	+	o	o	o	o	++	o	o	++
	Attend meetings	+	o	o	+	o	o	o	+	o
Water/ sanitation	Woman-headed household	—	*	o	o	o	o	o	o	o
	Attend meetings	o	*	++	+	o	+	o	+	+
Watershed	Woman-headed household	o	o	o	o	o	o	o	o	o
	Attend meetings	o	-	o	o	o	o	o	o	+

Source: Household questionnaire.

Functions: 1 = financing; 2 = staffing; 3 = provisioning; 4 = community-based action; 5 = capacity building; 6 = coordination of activities; 7 = M&E; 8 = conflict resolution/ accountability; 9 = information sharing/dissemination.

  + Significant positive association at 95 percent.

++ Significant positive association at 99 percent.

  - Significant negative association at 95 percent.

— Significant negative association at 99 percent.

  o No significant association.

  * Insufficient data. Relatively few local organizations undertook activities falling under the general function area of staffing. In the case of the drinking water and sanitation projects, in which this problem was particularly acute, this function has not been included in the analysis.

Table A17 Participation in Decision Making by Organizational Position, Women's Development and Empowerment Sector

(Percent)

Who appoints officeholders

	Karnataka					Madhya Pradesh				
Position	*Do not know*	*Not at all*	*Partially*	*To a large extent*	*N*	*Do not know*	*Not at all*	*Partially*	*To a large extent*	*N*
Members	1	2	4	93	552	2	2	8	88	486
Influential members	2	95	3	0	550	3	58	31	8	483
Influential nonmembers	3	94	2	1	550	5	86	9	1	483
Locals who initiate the organization become leaders	3	95	2	0	551	7	89	3	1	474
NGO/SO staff	3	55	30	12	548	7	59	28	6	465

Who participates in key decisions

State	*LO reps*	*All members*	*Dominant members*	*Rural elite*	*GP president*	*LO staff*	*Others*	*N*
Karnataka	12	84	2	0	0	1	1	547
Madhya Pradesh	6	92	1	0	0	1	1	470

Source: Household questionnaire.

Note: Because of differences in the structure of data sets for each sector, the information for this sector is presented in a slightly different format than information for the other two sectors. GP = gram panchayat; LO = local organization; NGO = nongovernmental organization; SO = support organization.

115

Table A18 Participation in Decision Making by Organizational Position, Drinking Water Supply and Sanitation Sector

(Percent)

	Karnataka					Uttaranchal				
	Do not know	Not at all	Partially	To a large extent	N	Do not know	Not at all	Partially	To a large extent	N
Who appoints officeholders										
Members	32	12	6	50	404	13	24	3	60	570
Influential members	36	46	15	3	403	12	59	26	3	570
Influential nonmembers	38	59	3	0	402	11	82	76	0	568
Locals who initiate the organization become leaders	39	54	6	1	394	13	85	2	0	569
The NGO/SO staff	33	57	8	2	397	12	40	35	13	568
GP	33	33	18	16	402	12	78	9	1	568
Who participates in key decisions										
Representatives of local organizations	25	48	20	7	568	9	34	34	23	557
All members	23	39	14	24	565	0	17	10	73	548
Dominant members	25	62	8	5	562	10	74	14	2	550
GP president	26	26	30	18	576	11	82	6	1	549
GP dominant members	26	44	20	9	565	10	86	4	0	548
Rural elites	26	54	12	8	574	10	74	14	3	546
NGO/SO staff	30	65	4	2	568	8	39	30	23	544

Source: Household questionnaire.

Note: GP = gram panchayat; NGO = nongovernmental organization; SO = support organization.

Table A19 Participation in Decision Making by Poverty Rank, Drinking Water Supply and Sanitation Sector

(Percent)

Who has the final say in important decisions (such as locating water supply points and setting user charges for water)	Karnataka			
	Very poor	Poor	Middle	Wealthy
Representative of a local organization	12.3	14.5	22.9	24.7
All the members	4.9	6.4	7.8	11.1
Dominant members in the group	2.5	7.7	9.2	4.9
GP president	9.0	16.4	24.8	19.8
GP dominant members	6.6	11.8	5.9	4.9
Rural elites	4.1	10.9	2.0	4.9
NGO/LD staff	0.8	2.7	3.3	8.6
GP secretary	12.3	8.2	7.8	8.6
Do not know/no response	47.5	21.4	16.3	12.3
Total respondents	122	220	153	81

Who has the final say in important decisions (such as locating water supply points and setting user charges for water)	Uttaranchal			
	Very poor	Poor	Middle	Wealthy
Representative of a local organization	49.7	44.7	48.9	45.6
All the members	9.8	10.6	16.3	15.6
Dominant members in the group	2.8	2.8	2.1	2.7
GP president	0.0	0.0	0.0	0.0
GP dominant members	0.0	0.0	0.0	0.0
Rural elites	0.0	0.0	0.0	0.0
NGO/LD staff	19.6	16.3	18.4	16.3
Do not know/no response	18.2	25.5	14.2	19.7
Total respondents	143	141	141	147

Source: Household questionnaire.

Note: GP = gram panchayat; LD = line department; NGO = nongovernmental organization.

Table A20 Participation in Decision Making by Organizational Position, Watershed Development Sector

(Percent)

	Karnataka					Uttaranchal				
	Do not know	Not at all	Partially	To a large extent	N	Do not know	Not at all	Partially	To a large extent	N
Who appoints officeholders										
Members	1	2	3	94	549	8	8	2	82	521
Influential members	2	84	13	1	549	8	51	38	3	519
Influential nonmembers	2	97	1	0	549	8	88	3	0	520
Locals who initiate the organization become leaders	3	95	2	0	549	9	88	2	1	520
The NGO/SO staff	2	47	46	5	549	9	74	14	3	517
Who participates in key decisions										
Representatives of a local organization	20	43	36	21	548	6	87	0	7	441
All members	0	17	10	73	548	5	21	1	73	440
Dominant members	0	88	11	1	548	5	95	0	0	441
GP president	0	99	1	0	548	6	94	0	0	393
GP dominant members										
Rural elites	1	99	0	0	547	5	95	0	0	441
NGO/LD staff	0	52	35	13	548	6	85	0	9	393

Source: Household questionnaire.

Note: GP = gram panchayat; LD = line department; NGO = nongovernmental organization; SO = support organization.

Table A21 Participation in Decision Making by Poverty Rank, Watershed Development Sector

(Percent)

Who has the final say in important decisions (such as deciding the location of checkdams, etc.)	Karnataka			
	Very poor	Poor	Middle	Wealthy
Representative of a local organization	12.6	13.9	10.3	9.8
All the members	46.0	31.5	39.4	32.1
Dominant members in the group	4.6	1.8	3.0	8.0
High-caste and rich people outside the local organization	0.0	0.0	0.5	0.0
GP president	0.0	0.0	0.0	0.0
NGO/LD staff	25.3	37.6	36.5	36.6
Do not know/no response	11.5	15.2	10.3	13.4
Total respondents	87	165	203	112

Who has the final say in important decisions (such as deciding the location of checkdams, etc.)	Uttaranchal			
	Very poor	Poor	Middle	Wealthy
Representative of a local organization	6.7	7.4	5.4	2.1
All the members	70.9	54.4	64.3	64.1
Dominant members in the group	0.0	3.4	1.6	0.7
High-caste and rich people outside the local organization	0.0	0.0	0.0	0.0
GP president	0.0	0.7	1.6	2.8
NGO/LD staff	6.0	10.7	5.4	2.1
Do not know/no response	16.4	23.5	21.7	28.2
Total respondents	134	149	129	142

Source: Household questionnaire.

Note: GP = gram panchayat; LD = line department; NGO = nongovernmental organization.

Table A22 Poisson Regression of Number of Loans Obtained by Sample Members

(See table A32)

Variable	
CBO-GI	—
CBO-NI	○
CBO-SI	○
Scheduled tribe	○
Backward caste	○
Forward caste	○
Minority	+
Poor	○
Middle	○
Wealthy	○
0 to 1 acre	○
1 to 2.5 acres	○
2.5 to 5 acres	○
5 to 10 acres	○
10+ acres	○
Woman	○
Madhya Pradesh	—

Source: Household questionnaire.

Note: CBO-PI, scheduled caste, very poor, and landless are the reference categories. CBO-GI = community-based organization (government-initiated); CBO-NI = community-based organization (NGO-initiated); CBO-PI = community-based organization (project-initiated); CBO-SI = community-based organization (self-initiated).

   + Significant positive association at 95 percent.
   ++ Significant positive association at 99 percent.
   - Significant negative association at 95 percent.
   — Significant negative association at 99 percent.
   ○ No significant association.

Table A23 Ordered Probit Results for Improved Access to Clean Drinking Water

(See table A32)

Variable	
Line department	o
Gram panchayat	o
Scheduled tribe	o
Backward caste	o
Forward caste	o
Minority	o
Poor	o
Middle	o
Wealthy	o
0 to 1 acre	o
1 to 2.5 acres	o
2.5 to 5 acres	o
5 to 10 acres	o
10+ acres	o
Woman	o
Uttaranchal	++

Source: Household questionnaire.

Note: CBO-PI, scheduled caste, very poor, and landless are the reference categories.
CBO-PI = community-based organization (project-initiated).
+   Significant positive association at 95 percent.
++   Significant positive association at 99 percent.
- Significant negative association at 95 percent.
— Significant negative association at 99 percent.
o No significant association.

Table A24 Ordered Probit Results for Provision of Sanitary Facilities

(See table A32)

Variable	
Line department	o
Gram panchayat	o
Scheduled tribe	o
Backward caste	o
Forward caste	o
Minority	o
Poor	o
Middle	o
Wealthy	o
0 to 1 acre	o
1 to 2.5 acres	o
2.5 to 5 acres	o
5 to 10 acres	o
10+ acres	o
Woman	o
Uttaranchal	o

Source: Household questionnaire.
Note: CBO-PI, scheduled caste, very poor, and landless are the reference categories.
CBO-PI = community-based organization (project-initiated).
+   Significant positive association at 95 percent.
++ Significant positive association at 99 percent.
-   Significant negative association at 95 percent.
—   Significant negative association at 99 percent.
o   No significant association.

Table A25 Members' Assessment of Their Local Organization's Performance in Preventing Soil Erosion and Water Loss, by Poverty Ranking

Poverty ranking	Poor (%)	Adequate (%)	Good (%)	N
Very poor	35	20	45	203
Poor	24	21	55	272
Middle	20	20	60	324
Wealthy	27	17	56	231
Mean across all rankings (N)	25 (262)	19 (201)	55 (567)	1,030

Source: Household questionnaire.

Table A26 Members' Assessment of Their Local Organization's Performance in Improving Agricultural Production, by Poverty Ranking

Poverty ranking	Poor (%)	Adequate (%)	Good (%)	N
Very poor	45	26	29	201
Poor	41	27	32	274
Middle	32	28	40	324
Wealthy	37	28	35	229
Average across all rankings (N)	38 (391)	27 (282)	35 (355)	1,029

Source: Household questionnaire.

Table A27 Members' Assessment of Their Local Organization's Performance in Preventing Soil Erosion and Water Loss, by Size of Operational Holding

Size of operational holding	Poor (%)	Adequate (%)	Good (%)	N
No cultivation	57	13	30	47
0 to 1 acre	39	24	37	170
1 to 2.5 acres	29	27	44	154
2.5 to 5 acres	27	21	52	210
5 to 10 acres	17	14	69	213
10+ acres	13	15	72	246
Average across all sizes (N)	26 (264)	19 (201)	55 (575)	1,040

Source: Household questionnaire.

Table A28 Members' Assessment of Their Local Organization's Performance in Improving Agricultural Production, by Size of Operational Holding

Size of operational holding	Poor (%)	Adequate (%)	Good (%)	N
No cultivation	73	9	18	45
0 to 1 acre	66	15	19	169
1 to 2.5 acres	44	31	25	153
2.5 to 5 acres	33	29	38	212
5 to 10 acres	26	30	44	214
10+ acres	22	34	44	246
Average across all sizes (N)	38 (394)	27 (284)	352 (361)	1,039

Source: Household questionnaire.

Table A29 Ordered Probit Results for Prevention of Soil Erosion and Water Loss

(See table A32)

Variable	
CBO-GI	○
Scheduled tribe	○
Backward caste	○
Forward caste	○
Minority	+
Poor	○
Middle	○
Wealthy	○
0 to 1 acre	○
1 to 2.5 acres	+
2.5 to 5 acres	+
5 to 10 acres	+ +
10+ acres	+ +
Woman	○
Uttaranchal	—

Source: Household questionnaire.

Note: CBO-PI, scheduled caste, very poor, and landless are the reference categories. CBO-GI = community-based organization (government-initiated); CBO-PI = community-based organization (project-initiated).

  +   Significant positive association at 95 percent.
 + + Significant positive association at 99 percent.
  -   Significant negative association at 95 percent.
  —   Significant negative association at 99 percent.
  ○   No significant association.

Table A30 Ordered Probit Results for Improvements in Agricultural Production

(See table A32)

Variable	
CBO-GI	○
Scheduled tribe	○
Backward caste	○
Forward caste	○
Minority	○
Poor	○
Middle	○
Wealthy	○
0 to 1 acre	○
1 to 2.5 acres	+ +
2.5 to 5 acres	+ +
5 to 10 acres	+ +
10+ acres	+ +
Woman	○
Uttaranchal	-

Source: Household questionnaire.

Note: CBO-PI, scheduled caste, very poor, and landless are the reference categories. CBO-GI = community-based organization (government-initiated); CBO-PI = community-based organization (project-initiated).

  + Significant positive association at 95 percent.
 + + Significant positive association at 99 percent.
  - Significant negative association at 95 percent.
 — Significant negative association at 99 percent.
  ○ No significant association.

Table A31 Age of the Sample Organizations by Sector

Year established	Women	Water/sanitation	Watershed	Total
1955	0	1	0	1
1965	0	1	0	1
1976	1	0	0	1
1984	0	4	0	4
1990	0	3	0	3
1992	1	0	0	1
1993	0	5	0	5
1995	0	6	0	6
1996	1	8	0	9
1997	1	6	0	7
1998	4	9	3	16
1999	9	10	17	36
2000	62	6	26	94
2001	31	1	19	51
2002	16	0	3	19
Total	126	60	68	254

Source: Local organization officials questionnaire.

Note: Accurate data on age were only available for 254 CBOs. Respondents least able to answer this question were found in the water and sanitation section. This reflects the fact, emphasized in the sector reports (Alsop 2004), that many CBO-GIs are more de facto than de jure. CBO = community-based organization; CBO-GI = community-based organization (government-initiated).

Table A32 Probit Estimation Results: Association between Assets, Processes, Linkages, Context, and Performance of Functions

Function	Variable	Coefficient	Robust standard error	z-value	p-value
Women's Development and Empowerment					
Financing (N = 606)					
	Human assets	0.10272	0.16232	0.63	0.527
	Material assets	0.14050	0.14692	0.96	0.339
	Financial assets	0.19439	0.13976	1.39	0.164
	Households attend meetings	0.17449	0.16023	1.09	0.276
	Always conducts self-monitoring	0.13986	0.13731	1.02	0.308
	Members aware of objectives	0.06459	0.14891	0.43	0.664
	Members aware of rules	0.45590	0.17944	2.54	0.011
	Representatives aware of rules	−0.20650	0.14849	−1.39	0.164
	Meeting minutes read	−0.03670	0.12304	−0.30	0.766
	Meeting minutes orally informed	−0.54715	0.18722	−2.92	0.003
	Meeting minutes available upon request	−0.22768	0.10957	−2.08	0.038
	Linkages with gram panchayats (KA)	−0.04484	0.14551	−0.31	0.758
	Linkages with gram panchayats (MP)	−0.13072	0.19697	−0.66	0.507
	Linkages with other local organizations (KA)	0.29717	0.14863	2.00	0.046
	Linkages with other local organizations (MP)	−0.05690	0.19725	−0.29	0.773
	Linkages with line department (KA)	−0.16161	0.16170	−1.00	0.318
	Linkages with line department (MP)	−1.22879	0.42834	−2.87	0.004
	Caste: scheduled tribe	0.34732	0.15673	2.22	0.027
	Caste: backward caste	0.35285	0.14073	2.51	0.012
	Caste: forward caste	0.28256	0.25521	1.11	0.268
	Caste: minority	0.45029	0.31148	1.45	0.148
	Poverty ranking: poor	−0.17538	0.13070	−1.34	0.180

(Table continues on the following pages.)

Table A32 (*continued*)

Function	Variable	Coefficient	Robust standard error	z-value	p-value
	Poverty ranking: middle	−0.07257	0.16078	−0.45	0.652
	Poverty ranking: wealthy	−0.45361	0.21856	−2.08	0.038
	Landholding: 0–1 acre	0.19149	0.15109	1.27	0.205
	Landholding: 1–2.5 acres	0.25098	0.15509	1.62	0.106
	Landholding: 2.5–5 acres	0.10380	0.15938	0.65	0.515
	Landholding: 5–10 acres	0.18956	0.19496	0.97	0.331
	Landholding: 10+ acres	0.34975	0.30405	1.15	0.250
	Woman-headed household	0.23599	0.13003	1.81	0.070
	Distance to market	−0.61067	0.08952	−6.82	0.000
	Irrigated land	0.07901	0.06358	1.24	0.214
	Number of households	0.20357	0.09933	2.05	0.040
	Project village	0.90798	0.17847	5.09	0.000
	Madhya Pradesh	−0.77370	0.26845	−2.88	0.004
	CBO-GI	0.39150	0.15150	2.58	0.010
	CBO-NI	0.49170	0.23126	2.13	0.033
	Constant: lower boundary	−0.50811	0.59354	−0.86	0.392
	Constant: upper boundary	0.60017	0.59016	1.02	0.309
Staffing (N = 161)					
	Human assets	−0.78298	0.48872	−1.60	0.109
	Material assets	0.41192	0.37619	1.09	0.274
	Financial assets	0.10065	0.32996	0.31	0.760
	Households attend meetings	0.76827	0.33500	2.29	0.022
	Always conducts self-monitoring	−0.35911	0.45159	−0.80	0.426
	Members aware of objectives	−0.50980	0.38347	−1.33	0.184
•	Members aware of rules	0.47928	0.54700	0.88	0.381
	Representatives aware of rules	0.09571	0.37934	0.25	0.801
	Meeting minutes read	−0.17521	0.35568	−0.49	0.622
	Meeting minutes orally informed	−0.95044	0.46313	−2.05	0.040
	Meeting minutes available upon request	0.26428	0.24510	1.08	0.281
	Linkages with gram panchayats (KA)	0.70725	0.62994	1.12	0.262
	Linkages with gram panchayats (MP)	−0.08165	0.42943	−0.19	0.849

Table A32 (*continued*)

Function	Variable	Coefficient	Robust standard error	z-value	p-value
	Linkages with other local organizations (KA)	0.25991	0.56025	0.46	0.643
	Linkages with other local organizations (MP)	0.95046	0.46963	2.02	0.043
	Caste: scheduled tribe	0.74393	0.40409	1.84	0.066
	Caste: backward caste	0.51359	0.44758	1.15	0.251
	Caste: forward caste	0.70807	0.55029	1.29	0.198
	Caste: minority	−1.94287	0.87658	−2.22	0.027
	Poverty ranking: poor	0.01923	0.27929	0.07	0.945
	Poverty ranking: middle	−0.05441	0.29440	−0.18	0.853
	Poverty ranking: wealthy	−1.16683	0.39941	−2.92	0.003
	Landholding: 0–1 acre	−0.22378	0.37058	−0.60	0.546
	Landholding: 1–2.5 acres	−0.09451	0.35132	−0.27	0.788
	Landholding: 2.5–5 acres	−0.07073	0.31711	−0.22	0.824
	Landholding: 5–10 acres	−0.31029	0.32241	−0.96	0.336
	Landholding: 10+ acres	−0.13040	0.57909	−0.23	0.822
	Woman-headed household	−0.02987	0.27219	−0.11	0.913
	Distance to market	−0.52220	0.23402	−2.23	0.026
	Irrigated land	0.30406	0.18345	1.66	0.097
	Number of households	0.76785	0.28032	2.74	0.006
	Project village	−0.07276	0.45989	−0.16	0.874
	Madhya Pradesh	−0.17754	0.84301	−0.21	0.833
	CBO-GI	−0.60335	0.42174	−1.43	0.153
	CBO-NI	−0.97504	1.06448	−0.92	0.360
	Constant: lower boundary	0.70962	1.71050	0.41	0.678
	Constant: upper boundary	2.33025	1.70798	1.36	0.172
Provisioning (N = 1,360)					
	Human assets	−0.06010	0.10204	−0.59	0.556
	Material assets	−0.11080	0.09229	−1.20	0.230
	Financial assets	−0.00910	0.09168	−0.10	0.921
	Households attend meetings	0.15933	0.10400	1.53	0.126
	Always conducts self-monitoring	0.05497	0.09286	0.59	0.554
	Members aware of objectives	0.12647	0.10236	1.24	0.217

(*Table continues on the following pages.*)

Table A32 (*continued*)

Function	Variable	Coefficient	Robust standard error	z-value	p-value
	Members aware of rules	0.36969	0.10121	3.65	0.000
	Representatives aware of rules	0.36051	0.09941	3.63	0.000
	Meeting minutes read	−0.11791	0.08839	−1.33	0.182
	Meeting minutes orally informed	−0.16185	0.11635	−1.39	0.164
	Meeting minutes available upon request	−0.11493	0.07309	−1.57	0.116
	Linkages with gram panchayats (KA)	0.09181	0.11403	0.81	0.421
	Linkages with gram panchayats (MP)	−0.39045	0.10949	−3.57	0.000
	Linkages with other local organizations (KA)	0.39775	0.10940	3.64	0.000
	Linkages with other local organizations (MP)	−0.10599	0.11471	−0.92	0.356
	Linkages with line department (KA)	−0.54690	0.15822	−3.46	0.001
	Linkages with line department (MP)	−0.33107	0.29131	−1.14	0.256
	Caste: scheduled tribe	0.26965	0.10395	2.59	0.009
	Caste: backward caste	0.23717	0.09894	2.40	0.017
	Caste: forward caste	0.54311	0.14670	3.70	0.000
	Caste: minority	0.19388	0.24983	0.78	0.438
	Poverty ranking: poor	−0.01684	0.09243	−0.18	0.855
	Poverty ranking: middle	−0.00685	0.10231	−0.07	0.947
	Poverty ranking: wealthy	−0.14965	0.12629	−1.18	0.236
	Landholding: 0–1 acre	−0.03020	0.12411	−0.24	0.808
	Landholding: 1–2.5 acres	−0.06440	0.10630	−0.61	0.545
	Landholding: 2.5–5 acres	−0.09576	0.11259	−0.85	0.395
	Landholding: 5–10 acres	0.01159	0.11945	0.10	0.923
	Landholding: 10+ acres	0.26178	0.15145	1.73	0.084
	Woman-headed household	−0.09707	0.08405	−1.15	0.248
	Distance to market	−0.15913	0.05724	−2.78	0.005
	Irrigated land	0.28380	0.04645	6.11	0.000
	Number of households	−0.19917	0.05909	−3.37	0.001
	Project village	0.27379	0.13358	2.05	0.040

Table A32 (continued)

Function	Variable	Coefficient	Robust standard error	z-value	p-value
	Madhya Pradesh	0.46838	0.16648	2.81	0.005
	CBO-GI	0.04951	0.10189	0.49	0.627
	CBO-NI	0.26086	0.18568	1.40	0.160
	Subfunction #6 dummy	−0.75925	0.09111	−8.33	0.000
	Subfunction #9 dummy	−1.33645	0.11795	−11.33	0.000
	Subfunction #10 dummy	−1.28996	0.21513	−6.00	0.000
	Subfunction #11 dummy	−1.10928	0.09851	−11.26	0.000
	Constant: lower boundary	−1.67547	0.39606	−4.23	0.000
	Constant: upper boundary	−0.58984	0.39509	−1.49	0.135
Community-based action (N = 256)					
	Human assets	0.33335	0.28318	1.18	0.239
	Material assets	−0.56693	0.27770	−2.04	0.041
	Financial assets	1.04176	0.32851	3.17	0.002
	Households attend meetings	0.41491	0.24275	1.71	0.087
	Always conducts self-monitoring	−0.19077	0.27637	−0.69	0.490
	Members aware of objectives	−0.65096	0.33517	−1.94	0.052
	Members aware of rules	0.23190	0.29125	0.80	0.426
	Representatives aware of rules	0.71988	0.27724	2.60	0.009
	Meeting minutes read	−0.33121	0.32290	−1.03	0.305
	Meeting minutes orally informed	−0.40397	0.29384	−1.37	0.169
	Meeting minutes available upon request	0.10382	0.18073	0.57	0.566
	Linkages with gram panchayats (KA)	1.59128	0.46691	3.41	0.001
	Linkages with gram panchayats (MP)	−0.28988	0.25680	−1.13	0.259
	Linkages with other local organizations (KA)	1.21399	0.46214	2.63	0.009
	Linkages with other local organizations (MP)	−0.05177	0.34986	−0.15	0.882
	Linkages with line department (KA)	−0.95150	0.50835	−1.87	0.061
	Linkages with line department (MP)	0.74283	0.64280	1.16	0.248

(Table continues on the following pages.)

Table A32 (*continued*)

Function	Variable	Coefficient	Robust standard error	z-value	p-value
	Caste: scheduled tribe	−0.06135	0.23416	−0.26	0.793
	Caste: backward caste	−0.01673	0.26431	−0.06	0.950
	Caste: forward caste	−0.63601	0.60087	−1.06	0.290
	Caste: minority	0.44120	1.29483	0.34	0.733
	Poverty ranking: poor	−0.30475	0.20074	−1.52	0.129
	Poverty ranking: middle	0.02229	0.22040	0.10	0.919
	Poverty ranking: wealthy	0.42958	0.34587	1.24	0.214
	Landholding: 0–1 acre	0.39799	0.29862	1.33	0.183
	Landholding: 1–2.5 acres	0.18411	0.23031	0.80	0.424
	Landholding: 2.5–5 acres	0.30267	0.25771	1.17	0.240
	Landholding: 5–10 acres	0.28091	0.31454	0.89	0.372
	Landholding: 10+ acres	0.42822	0.33393	1.28	0.200
	Woman-headed household	−0.18412	0.19350	−0.95	0.341
	Distance to market	−0.42724	0.18836	−2.27	0.023
	Irrigated land	0.38438	0.14657	2.62	0.009
	Number of households	0.42700	0.19467	2.19	0.028
	Project village	0.13736	0.41281	0.33	0.739
	Madhya Pradesh	1.14678	0.55078	2.08	0.037
	CBO-GI	0.04287	0.29486	0.15	0.884
	CBO-NI	0.15777	0.56708	0.28	0.781
	Subfunction #13 dummy	−0.05308	0.15432	−0.34	0.731
	Constant: lower boundary	2.35675	1.38272	1.70	0.088
	Constant: upper boundary	3.69875	1.38777	2.67	0.008
Capacity building (N = 1,946)					
	Human assets	0.08140	0.09874	0.82	0.410
	Material assets	−0.33509	0.07809	−4.29	0.000
	Financial assets	−0.03258	0.08965	−0.36	0.716
	Households attend meetings	0.09929	0.09968	1.00	0.319
	Always conducts self-monitoring	0.16955	0.08471	2.00	0.045
	Members aware of objectives	0.09110	0.09292	0.98	0.327
	Members aware of rules	0.34981	0.10295	3.40	0.001
	Representatives aware of rules	0.28217	0.09501	2.97	0.003
	Meeting minutes read	−0.01691	0.07858	−0.22	0.830

Table A32 *(continued)*

Function	Variable	Coefficient	Robust standard error	z-value	p-value
	Meeting minutes orally informed	−0.04610	0.11961	−0.39	0.700
	Meeting minutes available upon request	0.00843	0.06688	0.13	0.900
	Linkages with gram panchayats (KA)	0.19397	0.08502	2.28	0.023
	Linkages with gram panchayats (MP)	0.08945	0.12151	0.74	0.462
	Linkages with other local organizations (KA)	0.29374	0.09190	3.20	0.001
	Linkages with other local organizations (MP)	−0.10962	0.13304	−0.82	0.410
	Linkages with line department (KA)	−0.22402	0.10490	−2.14	0.033
	Linkages with line department (MP)	0.37631	0.30182	1.25	0.212
	Caste: scheduled tribe	0.02402	0.09332	0.26	0.797
	Caste: backward caste	0.18928	0.08963	2.11	0.035
	Caste: forward caste	0.22771	0.14760	1.54	0.123
	Caste: minority	0.17687	0.20743	0.85	0.394
	Poverty ranking: poor	−0.16911	0.08329	−2.03	0.042
	Poverty ranking: middle	−0.19213	0.09672	−1.99	0.047
	Poverty ranking: wealthy	−0.18923	0.15293	−1.24	0.216
	Landholding: 0–1 acre	−0.00136	0.10299	−0.01	0.989
	Landholding: 1–2.5 acres	0.05920	0.10177	0.58	0.561
	Landholding: 2.5–5 acres	−0.06151	0.10557	−0.58	0.560
	Landholding: 5–10 acres	−0.00040	0.11910	0.00	0.997
	Landholding: 10+ acres	−0.02294	0.17846	−0.13	0.898
	Woman-headed household	−0.02218	0.07980	−0.28	0.781
	Distance to market	−0.24353	0.06164	−3.95	0.000
	Irrigated land	0.29345	0.05180	5.66	0.000
	Number of households	0.04253	0.05731	0.74	0.458
	Project village	0.15795	0.12806	1.23	0.217
	Madhya Pradesh	−0.43026	0.17537	−2.45	0.014
	CBO-GI	0.24627	0.09109	2.70	0.007

(Table continues on the following pages.)

Table A32 (*continued*)

Function	Variable	Coefficient	Robust standard error	z-value	p-value
	CBO-NI	0.24112	0.17101	1.41	0.159
	Subfunction #16 dummy	0.85216	0.06872	12.40	0.000
	Subfunction #17 dummy	0.82052	0.07271	11.29	0.000
	Constant: lower boundary	−0.29636	0.36366	−0.81	0.415
	Constant: upper boundary	0.95202	0.37022	2.57	0.010
Coordination of activities (N = 866)					
	Human assets	0.12467	0.14402	0.87	0.387
	Material assets	0.00540	0.12927	0.04	0.967
	Financial assets	0.02274	0.13524	0.17	0.866
	Households attend meetings	−0.09978	0.11643	−0.86	0.391
	Always conducts self-monitoring	−0.03213	0.13438	−0.24	0.811
	Members aware of objectives	0.07367	0.12423	0.59	0.553
	Members aware of rules	0.29379	0.14125	2.08	0.038
	Representatives aware of rules	0.25320	0.12605	2.01	0.045
	Meeting minutes read	0.07559	0.12488	0.61	0.545
	Meeting minutes orally informed	−0.25382	0.16527	−1.54	0.125
	Meeting minutes available upon request	−0.14893	0.08917	−1.67	0.095
	Linkages with gram panchayats (KA)	−0.25598	0.18831	−1.36	0.174
	Linkages with gram panchayats (MP)	0.06924	0.13158	0.53	0.599
	Linkages with other local organizations (KA)	0.05105	0.18052	0.28	0.777
	Linkages with other local organizations (MP)	0.27148	0.14963	1.81	0.070
	Linkages with line department (KA)	0.22944	0.20774	1.10	0.269
	Linkages with line department (MP)	0.50039	0.58327	0.86	0.391
	Caste: scheduled tribe	0.13995	0.13625	1.03	0.304
	Caste: backward caste	0.17146	0.14324	1.20	0.231
	Caste: forward caste	0.59539	0.23909	2.49	0.013
	Caste: minority	0.77371	0.43598	1.77	0.076

Table A32 (*continued*)

Function	Variable	Coefficient	Robust standard error	z-value	p-value
	Poverty ranking: poor	−0.13537	0.10915	−1.24	0.215
	Poverty ranking: middle	0.10317	0.12160	0.85	0.396
	Poverty ranking: wealthy	0.04602	0.16902	0.27	0.785
	Landholding: 0–1 acre	−0.07650	0.16431	−0.47	0.642
	Landholding: 1–2.5 acres	−0.04398	0.13796	−0.32	0.750
	Landholding: 2.5–5 acres	0.07664	0.13172	0.58	0.561
	Landholding: 5–10 acres	0.13390	0.14086	0.95	0.342
	Landholding: 10+ acres	−0.03654	0.17919	−0.20	0.838
	Woman-headed household	0.24470	0.10315	2.37	0.018
	Distance to market	−0.09356	0.06447	−1.45	0.147
	Irrigated land	0.09462	0.04950	1.91	0.056
	Number of households	0.10201	0.08975	1.14	0.256
	Project village	0.50951	0.19124	2.66	0.008
	Madhya Pradesh	0.35020	0.25656	1.37	0.172
	CBO-GI	0.10771	0.14388	0.75	0.454
	CBO-NI	−0.21650	0.22452	−0.96	0.335
	Subfunction #18 dummy	−0.76125	0.09812	−7.76	0.000
	Subfunction #19 dummy	−0.88101	0.10758	−8.19	0.000
	Constant: lower boundary	0.17632	0.59280	0.30	0.766
	Constant: upper boundary	1.33481	0.59037	2.26	0.024
Monitoring and evaluation (N = 711)					
	Human assets	0.18398	0.15424	1.19	0.233
	Material assets	0.00147	0.13391	0.01	0.991
	Financial assets	0.14881	0.14761	1.01	0.313
	Households attend meetings	0.11657	0.15807	0.74	0.461
	Always conducts self-monitoring	0.22470	0.12389	1.81	0.070
	Members aware of objectives	−0.05884	0.14157	−0.42	0.678
	Members aware of rules	0.26186	0.16746	1.56	0.118
	Representatives aware of rules	0.05174	0.15221	0.34	0.734
	Meeting minutes read	−0.21279	0.12634	−1.68	0.092
	Meeting minutes orally informed	−0.01481	0.17212	−0.09	0.931

(*Table continues on the following pages.*)

Table A32 (*continued*)

Function	Variable	Coefficient	Robust standard error	z-value	p-value
	Meeting minutes available upon request	0.10180	0.10980	0.93	0.354
	Linkages with gram panchayats (KA)	−0.01876	0.13851	−0.14	0.892
	Linkages with gram panchayats (MP)	−0.07881	0.18057	−0.44	0.663
	Linkages with other local organizations (KA)	0.44597	0.15294	2.92	0.004
	Linkages with other local organizations (MP)	−0.43991	0.21032	−2.09	0.036
	Linkages with line department (KA)	0.39240	0.18693	2.10	0.036
	Linkages with line department (MP)	−0.63643	0.43243	−1.47	0.141
	Caste: scheduled tribe	0.00456	0.15289	0.03	0.976
	Caste: backward caste	0.32409	0.14005	2.31	0.021
	Caste: forward caste	0.41860	0.22284	1.88	0.060
	Caste: minority	−0.12043	0.29574	−0.41	0.684
	Poverty ranking: poor	−0.15408	0.13166	−1.17	0.242
	Poverty ranking: middle	−0.23196	0.14839	−1.56	0.118
	Poverty ranking: wealthy	−0.01557	0.21681	−0.07	0.943
	Landholding: 0–1 acre	−0.03502	0.17474	−0.20	0.841
	Landholding: 1–2.5 acres	−0.00549	0.15276	−0.04	0.971
	Landholding: 2.5–5 acres	0.15192	0.15783	0.96	0.336
	Landholding: 5–10 acres	0.05958	0.17571	0.34	0.735
	Landholding: 10+ acres	0.06611	0.26138	0.25	0.800
	Woman-headed household	0.13324	0.12106	1.10	0.271
	Distance to market	−0.36324	0.09621	−3.78	0.000
	Irrigated land	0.29826	0.08164	3.65	0.000
	Number of households	0.26789	0.09472	2.83	0.005
	Project village	0.36881	0.20057	1.84	0.066
	Madhya Pradesh	0.32539	0.26258	1.24	0.215
	CBO-GI	0.12602	0.15014	0.84	0.401
	CBO-NI	0.55705	0.28308	1.97	0.049
	Constant: lower boundary	−0.01026	0.58610	−0.02	0.986
	Constant: upper boundary	1.35405	0.59775	2.27	0.023

Table A32 *(continued)*

Function	Variable	Coefficient	Robust standard error	z-value	p-value
Conflict resolution and accountability (N = 1,388)					
	Human assets	0.39574	0.10767	3.68	0.000
	Material assets	−0.51027	0.09837	−5.19	0.000
	Financial assets	0.17246	0.10178	1.69	0.090
	Households attend meetings	0.19256	0.11066	1.74	0.082
	Always conducts self-monitoring	−0.00826	0.09816	−0.08	0.933
	Members aware of objectives	0.02854	0.10318	0.28	0.782
	Members aware of rules	0.14608	0.11657	1.25	0.210
	Representatives aware of rules	−0.01860	0.10347	−0.18	0.857
	Meeting minutes read	0.08944	0.09240	0.97	0.333
	Meeting minutes orally informed	−0.07956	0.14382	−0.55	0.580
	Meeting minutes available upon request	−0.11881	0.07927	−1.50	0.134
	Linkages with gram panchayats (KA)	0.09503	0.11486	0.83	0.408
	Linkages with gram panchayats (MP)	−0.19249	0.12545	−1.53	0.125
	Linkages with other local organizations (KA)	0.41001	0.11633	3.52	0.000
	Linkages with other local organizations (MP)	−0.08602	0.13681	−0.63	0.530
	Linkages with line department (KA)	0.08112	0.17000	0.48	0.633
	Linkages with line department (MP)	−0.23476	0.33817	−0.69	0.488
	Caste: scheduled tribe	0.33350	0.11471	2.91	0.004
	Caste: backward caste	0.14981	0.10422	1.44	0.151
	Caste: forward caste	0.36898	0.18522	1.99	0.046
	Caste: minority	0.16983	0.30061	0.56	0.572
	Poverty ranking: poor	−0.05619	0.09558	−0.59	0.557
	Poverty ranking: middle	−0.11387	0.10877	−1.05	0.295
	Poverty ranking: wealthy	−0.20747	0.18461	−1.12	0.261
	Landholding: 0–1 acre	0.09220	0.13565	0.68	0.497

(Table continues on the following pages.)

Table A32 *(continued)*

Function	Variable	Coefficient	Robust standard error	z-value	p-value
	Landholding: 1–2.5 acres	0.13057	0.11005	1.19	0.235
	Landholding: 2.5–5 acres	0.26329	0.11830	2.23	0.026
	Landholding: 5–10 acres	0.25935	0.13646	1.90	0.057
	Landholding: 10+ acres	0.12442	0.17322	0.72	0.473
	Woman-headed household	0.10783	0.09296	1.16	0.246
	Distance to market	−0.29809	0.06818	−4.37	0.000
	Irrigated land	0.20890	0.05038	4.15	0.000
	Number of households	0.12223	0.07151	1.71	0.087
	Project village	0.35718	0.13836	2.58	0.010
	Madhya Pradesh	−0.12310	0.19104	−0.64	0.519
	CBO-GI	0.05870	0.10761	0.55	0.585
	CBO-NI	0.02275	0.19293	0.12	0.906
	Subfunction #22 dummy	−1.65272	0.08896	−18.58	0.000
	Subfunction #23 dummy	−2.23559	0.10171	−21.98	0.000
	Constant: lower boundary	−1.21141	0.46771	−2.59	0.010
	Constant: upper boundary	0.03747	0.46268	0.08	0.935
Information sharing and dissemination (N = 496)					
	Human assets	0.15379	0.18153	0.85	0.397
	Material assets	0.08766	0.14502	0.60	0.546
	Financial assets	−0.17651	0.14500	−1.22	0.223
	Households attend meetings	−0.19267	0.15914	−1.21	0.226
	Always conducts self-monitoring	−0.02181	0.14520	−0.15	0.881
	Members aware of objectives	−0.17769	0.16300	−1.09	0.276
	Members aware of rules	0.74751	0.17371	4.30	0.000
	Representatives aware of rules	0.46811	0.15874	2.95	0.003
	Meeting minutes read	−0.15367	0.13316	−1.15	0.248
	Meeting minutes orally informed	0.59989	0.21449	2.80	0.005
	Meeting minutes available upon request	−0.33363	0.11454	−2.91	0.004
	Linkages with gram panchayats (KA)	0.12233	0.15345	0.80	0.425
	Linkages with gram panchayats (MP)	−0.39226	0.20454	−1.92	0.055

Table A32 (*continued*)

Function	Variable	Coefficient	Robust standard error	z-value	p-value
	Linkages with other local organizations (KA)	0.08685	0.15822	0.55	0.583
	Linkages with other local organizations (MP)	−0.19711	0.23701	−0.83	0.406
	Linkages with line department (KA)	0.48861	0.19314	2.53	0.011
	Linkages with line department (MP)	−0.03021	0.86836	−0.03	0.972
	Caste: scheduled tribe	0.14404	0.16289	0.88	0.377
	Caste: backward caste	−0.16468	0.15322	−1.07	0.282
	Caste: forward caste	−0.25230	0.22289	−1.13	0.258
	Caste: minority	0.52560	0.27999	1.88	0.060
	Poverty ranking: poor	0.13163	0.13534	0.97	0.331
	Poverty ranking: middle	−0.09037	0.17638	−0.51	0.608
	Poverty ranking: wealthy	0.29008	0.23800	1.22	0.223
	Landholding: 0–1 acre	0.10477	0.17972	0.58	0.560
	Landholding: 1–2.5 acres	−0.08880	0.16935	−0.52	0.600
	Landholding: 2.5–5 acres	0.26571	0.17140	1.55	0.121
	Landholding: 5–10 acres	−0.05386	0.20520	−0.26	0.793
	Landholding: 10+ acres	0.33265	0.27645	1.20	0.229
	Woman-headed household	0.30752	0.13848	2.22	0.026
	Distance to market	−0.42853	0.10939	−3.92	0.000
	Irrigated land	0.01177	0.08714	0.14	0.893
	Number of households	0.14032	0.10165	1.38	0.167
	Project village	−0.06654	0.19381	−0.34	0.731
	Madhya Pradesh	0.65148	0.32427	2.01	0.045
	CBO-GI	−0.21412	0.16332	−1.31	0.190
	CBO-NI	−0.06368	0.29760	−0.21	0.831
	Constant: lower boundary	−0.15089	0.71405	−0.21	0.833
	Constant: upper boundary	1.32229	0.71330	1.85	0.064
Drinking Water Supply and Sanitation Financing (N = 173)					
	Human assets	−0.08892	0.26895	−0.33	0.741
	Material assets	−0.64721	0.31386	−2.06	0.039
	Financial assets	0.90177	0.30376	2.97	0.003

(*Table continues on the following pages.*)

Table A32 (*continued*)

Function	Variable	Coefficient	Robust standard error	z-value	p-value
	Households attend meetings	0.04596	0.28359	0.16	0.871
	Always conducts self-monitoring	−0.61098	0.30044	−2.03	0.042
	Members aware of objectives	1.12871	0.30088	3.75	0.000
	Members aware of rules	−0.21349	0.33213	−0.64	0.520
	Representatives aware of rules	0.39605	0.33671	1.18	0.240
	Meeting minutes read	−0.15259	0.25973	−0.59	0.557
	Meeting minutes orally informed	−0.16317	0.27563	−0.59	0.554
	Meeting minutes available upon request	−0.20514	0.24603	−0.83	0.404
	Linkages with gram panchayats	−0.19407	0.56768	−0.34	0.732
	Linkages with other local organizations	−0.15246	0.33989	−0.45	0.654
	Linkages with line department	−1.81792	0.86825	−2.09	0.036
	Caste: scheduled tribe	−0.41225	0.45004	−0.92	0.360
	Caste: backward caste	−0.53707	0.36996	−1.45	0.147
	Caste: forward caste	−0.26401	0.26209	−1.01	0.314
	Caste: minority	−0.58496	0.31735	−1.84	0.065
	Poverty ranking: poor	−0.32322	0.29954	−1.08	0.281
	Poverty ranking: middle	−0.43849	0.29348	−1.49	0.135
	Poverty ranking: wealthy	−0.18801	0.32229	−0.58	0.560
	Landholding: 0–1 acre	−0.02730	0.38138	−0.07	0.943
	Landholding: 1–2.5 acres	−0.32498	0.45909	−0.71	0.479
	Landholding: 2.5–5 acres	−0.37839	0.34711	−1.09	0.276
	Landholding: 5–10 acres	−0.15421	0.47843	−0.32	0.747
	Landholding: 10+ acres	−0.37913	0.45618	−0.83	0.406
	Woman-headed household	−1.00958	0.31679	−3.19	0.001
	Distance to market	0.30389	0.17649	1.72	0.085
	Irrigated land	−0.66375	0.18442	−3.60	0.000
	Number of households	0.01065	0.20777	0.05	0.959
	Uttaranchal	−1.50918	1.14269	−1.32	0.187
	Line department	1.33769	0.84482	1.58	0.113
	Gram panchayat	−0.88048	0.45990	−1.91	0.056
	Local organization has no officials	−2.41034	0.94248	−2.56	0.011

Table A32 (*continued*)

Function	Variable	Coefficient	Robust standard error	z-value	p-value
	Constant: lower boundary	−3.77168	2.09534	−1.80	0.072
	Constant: upper boundary	−1.02155	2.09625	−0.49	0.626
Provisioning (N = 1133)					
	Human assets	−0.25189	0.10790	−2.33	0.020
	Material assets	0.05325	0.09564	0.56	0.578
	Financial assets	0.22870	0.09938	2.30	0.021
	Households attend meetings	0.28037	0.11239	2.49	0.013
	Always conducts self-monitoring	−0.19022	0.10569	−1.80	0.072
	Members aware of objectives	0.35343	0.11016	3.21	0.001
	Members aware of rules	0.73136	0.15055	4.86	0.000
	Representatives aware of rules	−0.42307	0.10823	−3.91	0.000
	Meeting minutes read	0.36633	0.11706	3.13	0.002
	Meeting minutes orally informed	−0.12424	0.10553	−1.18	0.239
	Meeting minutes available upon request	−0.01471	0.09087	−0.16	0.871
	Linkages with gram panchayats	−0.37550	0.16136	−2.33	0.020
	Linkages with other local organizations	0.08376	0.13572	0.62	0.537
	Linkages with line department	−0.12774	0.16803	−0.76	0.447
	Caste: scheduled tribe	−0.49879	0.20970	−2.38	0.017
	Caste: backward caste	−0.03047	0.15176	−0.20	0.841
	Caste: forward caste	−0.10415	0.13519	−0.77	0.441
	Caste: minority	−0.12403	0.18781	−0.66	0.509
	Poverty ranking: poor	−0.16882	0.11308	−1.49	0.135
	Poverty ranking: middle	0.08222	0.12994	0.63	0.527
	Poverty ranking: wealthy	−0.03543	0.13538	−0.26	0.794
	Landholding: 0–1 acre	0.05529	0.14692	0.38	0.707
	Landholding: 1–2.5 acres	−0.05834	0.16002	−0.36	0.715
	Landholding: 2.5–5 acres	0.11728	0.13700	0.86	0.392
	Landholding: 5–10 acres	−0.19927	0.18326	−1.09	0.277

(*Table continues on the following pages.*)

Table A32 *(continued)*

Function	Variable	Coefficient	Robust standard error	z-value	p-value
	Landholding: 10+ acres	−0.08933	0.18048	−0.49	0.621
	Woman-headed household	−0.09232	0.09797	−0.94	0.346
	Distance to market	0.09259	0.05240	1.77	0.077
	Irrigated land	0.02518	0.05142	0.49	0.624
	Number of households	0.28605	0.08961	3.19	0.001
	Uttaranchal	1.03822	0.32518	3.19	0.001
	Line department	0.19144	0.31087	0.62	0.538
	Gram panchayat	−0.35903	0.16817	−2.13	0.033
	Local organization has no officials	0.05029	0.38719	0.13	0.897
	Subfunction #6 dummy	−0.50816	0.12244	−4.15	0.000
	Subfunction #9 dummy	−0.20139	0.25577	−0.79	0.431
	Subfunction #10 dummy	−0.70182	0.12477	−5.62	0.000
	Subfunction #11 dummy	−0.23584	0.08044	−2.93	0.003
	Constant: lower boundary	1.47125	0.71053	2.07	0.038
	Constant: upper boundary	3.27916	0.71629	4.58	0.000
Community-based action (N = 452)					
	Human assets	−0.19417	0.16662	−1.17	0.244
	Material assets	0.29824	0.15087	1.98	0.048
	Financial assets	−0.13852	0.18593	−0.75	0.456
	Households attend meetings	0.31832	0.14535	2.19	0.029
	Always conducts self-monitoring	−0.42373	0.17545	−2.42	0.016
	Members aware of objectives	0.48242	0.18899	2.55	0.011
	Members aware of rules	0.36935	0.26183	1.41	0.158
	Representatives aware of rules	−0.54645	0.19425	−2.81	0.005
	Meeting minutes read	0.16912	0.17639	0.96	0.338
	Meeting minutes orally informed	−0.06653	0.16269	−0.41	0.683
	Meeting minutes available upon request	0.18366	0.12747	1.44	0.150
	Linkages with gram panchayats	−1.59073	0.57363	−2.77	0.006
	Linkages with other local organizations	0.61422	0.20059	3.06	0.002

Table A32 (*continued*)

Function	Variable	Coefficient	Robust standard error	z-value	p-value
	Linkages with line department	−1.84671	0.37180	−4.97	0.000
	Caste: scheduled tribe	−1.21483	0.31734	−3.83	0.000
	Caste: backward caste	−0.53201	0.21472	−2.48	0.013
	Caste: forward caste	−0.37445	0.19717	−1.90	0.058
	Caste: minority	−0.78731	0.29846	−2.64	0.008
	Poverty ranking: poor	0.08312	0.15800	0.53	0.599
	Poverty ranking: middle	−0.09939	0.17634	−0.56	0.573
	Poverty ranking: wealthy	−0.01358	0.21106	−0.06	0.949
	Landholding: 0–1 acre	0.04410	0.19643	0.22	0.822
	Landholding: 1–2.5 acres	−0.27752	0.24365	−1.14	0.255
	Landholding: 2.5–5 acres	−0.05196	0.19065	−0.27	0.785
	Landholding: 5–10 acres	−0.15605	0.26326	−0.59	0.553
	Landholding: 10+ acres	0.00215	0.25817	0.01	0.993
	Woman-headed household	0.04059	0.16854	0.24	0.810
	Distance to market	−0.24241	0.08847	−2.74	0.006
	Irrigated land	0.03835	0.08279	0.46	0.643
	Number of households	0.51175	0.14433	3.55	0.000
	Uttaranchal	−0.43424	0.52780	−0.82	0.411
	Line department	0.22279	0.43224	0.52	0.606
	Gram panchayat	−0.62973	0.20217	−3.11	0.002
	Local organization has no officials	−0.44576	0.55326	−0.81	0.420
	Subfunction #13 dummy	0.12791	0.13368	0.96	0.339
	Constant: lower boundary	−1.30447	1.32183	−0.99	0.324
	Constant: upper boundary	0.76652	1.31851	0.58	0.561
Capacity building (N = 1,050)					
	Human assets	−0.26245	0.11414	−2.30	0.021
	Material assets	0.16488	0.11282	1.46	0.144
	Financial assets	0.17837	0.10010	1.78	0.075
	Households attend meetings	0.04905	0.10080	0.49	0.627
	Always conducts self-monitoring	−0.43366	0.10192	−4.25	0.000
	Members aware of objectives	−0.28445	0.10585	−2.69	0.007
	Members aware of rules	0.93579	0.13138	7.12	0.000

(*Table continues on the following pages.*)

Table A32 (*continued*)

Function	Variable	Coefficient	Robust standard error	z-value	p-value
	Representatives aware of rules	−0.40887	0.10218	−4.00	0.000
	Meeting minutes read	0.13223	0.11131	1.19	0.235
	Meeting minutes orally informed	−0.03036	0.11234	−0.27	0.787
	Meeting minutes available upon request	−0.04339	0.09118	−0.48	0.634
	Linkages with gram panchayats	0.45054	0.14658	3.07	0.002
	Linkages with other local organizations	−0.02651	0.12666	−0.21	0.834
	Linkages with line department	0.29235	0.16958	1.72	0.085
	Caste: scheduled tribe	−0.22058	0.22907	−0.96	0.336
	Caste: backward caste	−0.26097	0.15602	−1.67	0.094
	Caste: forward caste	−0.08342	0.13958	−0.60	0.550
	Caste: minority	−0.12335	0.16152	−0.76	0.445
	Poverty ranking: poor	−0.23052	0.11644	−1.98	0.048
	Poverty ranking: middle	0.03336	0.12027	0.28	0.781
	Poverty ranking: wealthy	−0.25163	0.13300	−1.89	0.058
	Landholding: 0–1 acre	0.21521	0.15645	1.38	0.169
	Landholding: 1–2.5 acres	0.14619	0.15149	0.97	0.335
	Landholding: 2.5–5 acres	0.11187	0.15668	0.71	0.475
	Landholding: 5–10 acres	0.06218	0.19287	0.32	0.747
	Landholding: 10+ acres	0.35213	0.17573	2.00	0.045
	Woman-headed household	−0.10966	0.10219	−1.07	0.283
	Distance to market	0.14716	0.04932	2.98	0.003
	Irrigated land	0.01426	0.05119	0.28	0.781
	Number of households	0.36957	0.09389	3.94	0.000
	Uttaranchal	1.98440	0.34931	5.68	0.000
	Line department	−0.90821	0.51816	−1.75	0.080
	Gram panchayat	−0.47559	0.14379	−3.31	0.001
	Local organization has no officials	0.56229	0.55891	1.01	0.314
	Subfunction #16 dummy	0.17954	0.15765	1.14	0.255
	Subfunction #17 dummy	0.79662	0.16521	4.82	0.000
	Constant: lower boundary	3.21451	0.75309	4.27	0.000
	Constant: upper boundary	4.99620	0.75538	6.61	0.000

Table A32 (*continued*)

Function	Variable	Coefficient	Robust standard error	z-value	p-value
Coordination of activities (N = 515)					
	Human assets	−0.41843	0.17815	−2.35	0.019
	Material assets	0.13122	0.20493	0.64	0.522
	Financial assets	0.38164	0.18610	2.05	0.040
	Households attend meetings	0.44661	0.17376	2.57	0.010
	Always conducts self-monitoring	−0.48596	0.17716	−2.74	0.006
	Members aware of objectives	0.09760	0.19890	0.49	0.624
	Members aware of rules	0.88536	0.24647	3.59	0.000
	Representatives aware of rules	−0.00438	0.22208	−0.02	0.984
	Meeting minutes read	0.74793	0.20174	3.71	0.000
	Meeting minutes orally informed	−0.21060	0.19694	−1.07	0.285
	Meeting minutes available upon request	−0.17753	0.16196	−1.10	0.273
	Linkages with gram panchayats	−0.41853	0.28325	−1.48	0.140
	Linkages with other local organizations	0.49664	0.19483	2.55	0.011
	Linkages with line department	0.36005	0.34497	1.04	0.297
	Caste: scheduled tribe	−0.06541	0.31286	−0.21	0.834
	Caste: backward caste	−0.52317	0.24945	−2.10	0.036
	Caste: forward caste	−0.48028	0.21124	−2.27	0.023
	Caste: minority	−0.44855	0.28315	−1.58	0.113
	Poverty ranking: poor	0.14003	0.18174	0.77	0.441
	Poverty ranking: middle	−0.14962	0.18401	−0.81	0.416
	Poverty ranking: wealthy	0.23417	0.22221	1.05	0.292
	Landholding: 0–1 acre	−0.13616	0.23591	−0.58	0.564
	Landholding: 1–2.5 acres	0.00356	0.26000	0.01	0.989
	Landholding: 2.5–5 acres	−0.28542	0.23042	−1.24	0.215
	Landholding: 5–10 acres	−0.72807	0.31376	−2.32	0.020
	Landholding: 10+ acres	−0.16704	0.29080	−0.57	0.566
	Woman-headed household	−0.35928	0.16603	−2.16	0.030
	Distance to market	0.15654	0.08686	1.80	0.072
	Irrigated land	−0.07157	0.09646	−0.74	0.458

(Table continues on the following pages.)

Table A32 (*continued*)

Function	Variable	Coefficient	Robust standard error	z-value	p-value
	Number of households	0.29554	0.13331	2.22	0.027
	Uttaranchal	1.58352	0.71679	2.21	0.027
	Line department	0.83484	0.45892	1.82	0.069
	Gram panchayat	−0.06285	0.22217	−0.28	0.777
	Local organization has no officials	−0.60881	0.69206	−0.88	0.379
	Subfunction #18 dummy	−0.52366	0.16902	−3.10	0.002
	Subfunction #19 dummy	−0.32594	0.14206	−2.29	0.022
	Constant: lower boundary	1.59135	1.33428	1.19	0.233
	Constant: upper boundary	3.97705	1.34400	2.96	0.003
Monitoring and evaluation (N = 365)					
	Human assets	−0.33897	0.21355	−1.59	0.112
	Material assets	0.51083	0.20575	2.48	0.013
	Financial assets	0.03842	0.18998	0.20	0.840
	Households attend meetings	0.19505	0.14929	1.31	0.191
	Always conducts self-monitoring	0.27207	0.17293	1.57	0.116
	Members aware of objectives	−0.61769	0.21404	−2.89	0.004
	Members aware of rules	0.74046	0.23118	3.20	0.001
	Representatives aware of rules	−0.73002	0.19374	−3.77	0.000
	Meeting minutes read	−0.14450	0.17597	−0.82	0.412
	Meeting minutes orally informed	0.33634	0.21254	1.58	0.114
	Meeting minutes available upon request	−0.16103	0.15651	−1.03	0.304
	Linkages with gram panchayats	−0.40752	0.24341	−1.67	0.094
	Linkages with other local organizations	1.32391	0.24800	5.34	0.000
	Linkages with line department	0.33432	0.19799	1.69	0.091
	Caste: scheduled tribe	−0.63698	0.36098	−1.76	0.078
	Caste: backward caste	−0.31732	0.30477	−1.04	0.298
	Caste: forward caste	0.28352	0.23794	1.19	0.233
	Caste: minority	−0.71317	0.42719	−1.67	0.095
	Poverty ranking: poor	−0.45340	0.17967	−2.52	0.012

Table A32 (continued)

Function	Variable	Coefficient	Robust standard error	z-value	p-value
	Poverty ranking: middle	−0.34202	0.18323	−1.87	0.062
	Poverty ranking: wealthy	−0.20531	0.18968	−1.08	0.279
	Landholding: 0–1 acre	0.08287	0.26691	0.31	0.756
	Landholding: 1–2.5 acres	−0.28828	0.27430	−1.05	0.293
	Landholding: 2.5–5 acres	−0.20561	0.28794	−0.71	0.475
	Landholding: 5–10 acres	−0.42284	0.36278	−1.17	0.244
	Landholding: 10+ acres	−0.37605	0.31997	−1.18	0.240
	Woman-headed household	−0.14388	0.16106	−0.89	0.372
	Distance to market	0.38911	0.09635	4.04	0.000
	Irrigated land	0.09442	0.10665	0.89	0.376
	Number of households	0.32307	0.18840	1.71	0.086
	Uttaranchal	2.53760	0.60501	4.19	0.000
	Line department	0.20892	0.38946	0.54	0.592
	Gram panchayat	−0.56940	0.35317	−1.61	0.107
	Local organization has no officials	−0.60570	0.56824	−1.07	0.286
	Constant: lower boundary	2.80631	1.30278	2.15	0.031
	Constant: upper boundary	5.04195	1.32400	3.81	0.000
Conflict resolution and accountability (N = 683)					
	Human assets	0.17923	0.14008	1.28	0.201
	Material assets	0.23026	0.12239	1.88	0.060
	Financial assets	−0.00156	0.13464	−0.01	0.991
	Households attend meetings	0.22377	0.11697	1.91	0.056
	Always conducts self-monitoring	−0.00790	0.12218	−0.06	0.948
	Members aware of objectives	−0.13457	0.12626	−1.07	0.287
	Members aware of rules	0.71588	0.20468	3.50	0.000
	Representatives aware of rules	−0.73794	0.15564	−4.74	0.000
	Meeting minutes read	0.49131	0.13451	3.65	0.000
	Meeting minutes orally informed	−0.18172	0.14994	−1.21	0.226
	Meeting minutes available upon request	−0.04139	0.11578	−0.36	0.721

(Table continues on the following pages.)

Table A32 (continued)

Function	Variable	Coefficient	Robust standard error	z-value	p-value
	Linkages with gram panchayats	−0.88378	0.20014	−4.42	0.000
	Linkages with other local organizations	0.13291	0.16775	0.79	0.428
	Linkages with line department	1.29634	0.17177	7.55	0.000
	Caste: scheduled tribe	−0.35106	0.28693	−1.22	0.221
	Caste: backward caste	−0.10349	0.21524	−0.48	0.631
	Caste: forward caste	−0.26072	0.18843	−1.38	0.166
	Caste: minority	−0.40473	0.28351	−1.43	0.153
	Poverty ranking: poor	−0.18809	0.14035	−1.34	0.180
	Poverty ranking: middle	−0.08362	0.13958	−0.60	0.549
	Poverty ranking: wealthy	−0.13406	0.14364	−0.93	0.351
	Landholding: 0–1 acre	0.35944	0.20393	1.76	0.078
	Landholding: 1–2.5 acres	0.13743	0.20894	0.66	0.511
	Landholding: 2.5–5 acres	0.39424	0.21435	1.84	0.066
	Landholding: 5–10 acres	−0.08839	0.27744	−0.32	0.750
	Landholding: 10+ acres	0.37619	0.22626	1.66	0.096
	Woman-headed household	−0.21363	0.14366	−1.49	0.137
	Distance to market	0.16526	0.06741	2.45	0.014
	Irrigated land	0.20326	0.07977	2.55	0.011
	Number of households	0.80854	0.11923	6.78	0.000
	Uttaranchal	3.45003	0.42782	8.06	0.000
	Line department	−0.61951	0.30138	−2.06	0.040
	Gram panchayat	0.05628	0.27250	0.21	0.836
	Local organization has no officials	1.02717	0.45534	2.26	0.024
	Subfunction #22 dummy	−0.38800	0.12940	−3.00	0.003
	Subfunction #23 dummy	−0.39624	0.11581	−3.42	0.001
	Constant: lower boundary	5.80682	0.97690	5.94	0.000
	Constant: upper boundary	7.83676	0.99698	7.86	0.000
Information sharing and dissemination (N = 425)					
	Human assets	−0.03243	0.15843	−0.20	0.838
	Material assets	0.01628	0.15242	0.11	0.915
	Financial assets	−0.08380	0.15373	−0.55	0.586
	Households attend meetings	0.30914	0.15756	1.96	0.050

Table A32 (*continued*)

Function	Variable	Coefficient	Robust standard error	z-value	p-value
	Always conducts self-monitoring	0.02093	0.16423	0.13	0.899
	Members aware of objectives	0.46808	0.15333	3.05	0.002
	Members aware of rules	0.09141	0.16284	0.56	0.575
	Representatives aware of rules	−0.69749	0.18417	−3.79	0.000
	Meeting minutes read	−0.09666	0.16969	−0.57	0.569
	Meeting minutes orally informed	0.29078	0.16444	1.77	0.077
	Meeting minutes available upon request	0.17282	0.14017	1.23	0.218
	Linkages with gram panchayats	0.29218	0.33212	0.88	0.379
	Linkages with other local organizations	0.09713	0.21454	0.45	0.651
	Linkages with line department	1.56005	0.28138	5.54	0.000
	Caste: scheduled tribe	−0.71083	0.28409	−2.50	0.012
	Caste: backward caste	−0.61085	0.22881	−2.67	0.008
	Caste: forward caste	−0.39453	0.20500	−1.92	0.054
	Caste: minority	−0.85459	0.25693	−3.33	0.001
	Poverty ranking: poor	0.15876	0.16477	0.96	0.335
	Poverty ranking: middle	0.42129	0.18086	2.33	0.020
	Poverty ranking: wealthy	0.02519	0.19097	0.13	0.895
	Landholding: 0–1 acre	0.65467	0.22371	2.93	0.003
	Landholding: 1–2.5 acres	0.77088	0.23054	3.34	0.001
	Landholding: 2.5–5 acres	0.41041	0.20826	1.97	0.049
	Landholding: 5–10 acres	0.40833	0.28582	1.43	0.153
	Landholding: 10+ acres	0.72298	0.26794	2.70	0.007
	Woman-headed household	0.19802	0.18180	1.09	0.276
	Distance to market	0.26886	0.08877	3.03	0.002
	Irrigated land	0.00427	0.07710	0.06	0.956
	Number of households	0.47885	0.13369	3.58	0.000
	Uttaranchal	2.88938	0.49059	5.89	0.000
	Line department	−0.87455	0.48230	−1.81	0.070
	Gram panchayat	−0.40843	0.26020	−1.57	0.116

(*Table continues on the following pages.*)

Table A32 (continued)

Function	Variable	Coefficient	Robust standard error	z-value	p-value
	Local organization has no officials	0.81481	0.55233	1.48	0.140
	Constant: lower boundary	5.32127	1.02914	5.17	0.000
	Constant: upper boundary	7.26739	1.05474	6.89	0.000

Watershed Development

Financing (N = 546)

	Human assets	−0.82434	0.20266	−4.07	0.000
	Material assets	−1.05439	0.18264	−5.77	0.000
	Financial assets	1.58275	0.19705	8.03	0.000
	Households attend meetings	0.12120	0.13827	0.88	0.381
	Always conducts self-monitoring	0.48179	0.22604	2.13	0.033
	Members aware of objectives	0.05041	0.23395	0.22	0.829
	Members aware of rules	0.25584	0.24581	1.04	0.298
	Representatives aware of rules	0.04561	0.15427	0.30	0.767
	Meeting minutes read	−0.09125	0.14235	−0.64	0.522
	Meeting minutes orally informed	0.30864	0.22919	1.35	0.178
	Meeting minutes available upon request	0.17283	0.18274	0.95	0.344
	Linkages with gram panchayats (KA)	0.56202	0.34251	1.64	0.101
	Linkages with gram panchayats (UA)	−0.08126	0.27973	−0.29	0.771
	Linkages with other local organizations (KA)	−0.23098	0.23806	−0.97	0.332
	Linkages with other local organizations (UA)	−1.44468	0.28047	−5.15	0.000
	Linkages with line department (KA)	0.68020	0.32299	2.11	0.035
	Linkages with line department (UA)	1.20192	0.28976	4.15	0.000
	Caste: scheduled tribe	−0.13393	0.27766	−0.48	0.630
	Caste: backward caste	0.50466	0.25901	1.95	0.051
	Caste: forward caste	0.41512	0.23519	1.77	0.078

Table A32 (*continued*)

Function	Variable	Coefficient	Robust standard error	z-value	p-value
	Caste: minority	1.19373	0.45235	2.64	0.008
	Poverty ranking: poor	0.17767	0.17106	1.04	0.299
	Poverty ranking: middle	0.11770	0.16485	0.71	0.475
	Poverty ranking: wealthy	0.22645	0.17379	1.30	0.193
	Landholding: 0–1 acre	0.11082	0.28394	0.39	0.696
	Landholding: 1–2.5 acres	0.16901	0.27078	0.62	0.533
	Landholding: 2.5–5 acres	−0.07790	0.23644	−0.33	0.742
	Landholding: 5–10 acres	0.00491	0.23833	0.02	0.984
	Landholding: 10+ acres	0.35118	0.24636	1.43	0.154
	Woman-headed household	0.02929	0.16771	0.17	0.861
	Distance to market	0.76191	0.10874	7.01	0.000
	Irrigated land	−0.12037	0.03215	−3.74	0.000
	Number of households	0.24105	0.12515	1.93	0.054
	Uttaranchal	2.12735	0.54726	3.89	0.000
	CBO-GI	−1.17614	0.22305	−5.27	0.000
	Constant: lower boundary	4.16455	0.86781	4.80	0.000
	Constant: lower boundary	6.02350	0.88250	6.83	0.000
Staffing (N = 160)					
	Human assets	−2.92485	1.16392	−2.51	0.012
	Material assets	−2.68677	1.49358	−1.80	0.072
	Financial assets	4.24796	1.06833	3.98	0.000
	Households attend meetings	−0.69856	0.25528	−2.74	0.006
	Always conducts self-monitoring	0.12200	0.53882	0.23	0.821
	Members aware of objectives	−1.72179	0.69598	−2.47	0.013
	Members aware of rules	−6.88911	2.29640	−3.00	0.003
	Representatives aware of rules	0.51615	0.53351	0.97	0.333
	Meeting minutes read	−0.16893	0.32757	−0.52	0.606
	Meeting minutes orally informed	−0.59588	0.52640	−1.13	0.258
	Meeting minutes available upon request	0.09522	0.31670	0.30	0.764

(Table continues on the following pages.)

Table A32 (continued)

Function	Variable	Coefficient	Robust standard error	z-value	p-value
	Linkages with gram panchayats (KA)	−0.77647	0.61123	−1.27	0.204
	Linkages with gram panchayats (UA)	4.07745	1.63872	2.49	0.013
	Linkages with other local organizations (KA)	0.67060	0.48820	1.37	0.170
	Linkages with other local organizations (UA)	−3.18872	1.34780	−2.37	0.018
	Linkages with line department (KA)	2.29971	0.82372	2.79	0.005
	Linkages with line department (UA)	3.67219	1.08179	3.39	0.001
	Caste: scheduled tribe	0.76044	0.56070	1.36	0.175
	Caste: backward caste	−0.48248	0.53183	−0.91	0.364
	Caste: forward caste	0.58826	0.39534	1.49	0.137
	Caste: minority	−1.00464	0.88110	−1.14	0.254
	Poverty ranking: poor	−0.51325	0.39764	−1.29	0.197
	Poverty ranking: middle	0.23066	0.34144	0.68	0.499
	Poverty ranking: wealthy	0.45651	0.35558	1.28	0.199
	Landholding: 0–1 acre	−0.03712	0.42511	−0.09	0.930
	Landholding: 1–2.5 acres	−0.03155	0.54608	−0.06	0.954
	Landholding: 2.5–5 acres	−0.18048	0.49798	−0.36	0.717
	Landholding: 5–10 acres	−0.42857	0.45760	−0.94	0.349
	Landholding: 10+ acres	−0.85708	0.52663	−1.63	0.104
	Woman-headed household	0.45597	0.35897	1.27	0.204
	Distance to market	0.13407	0.46915	0.29	0.775
	Irrigated land	−0.08326	0.11768	−0.71	0.479
	Number of households	1.73951	0.34362	5.06	0.000
	Uttaranchal	−0.43264	1.84323	−0.23	0.814
	CBO-GI	−1.90054	0.68826	−2.76	0.006
	Constant: lower boundary	−1.68512	2.87793	−0.59	0.558
	Constant: upper boundary	1.58726	2.91263	0.54	0.586
Provisioning (N = 1,201)					
	Human assets	0.03972	0.13017	0.31	0.760
	Material assets	−0.63250	0.11321	−5.59	0.000

Table A32 (*continued*)

Function	Variable	Coefficient	Robust standard error	z-value	p-value
	Financial assets	0.63112	0.09528	6.62	0.000
	Households attend meetings	0.00820	0.08329	0.10	0.922
	Always conducts self-monitoring	0.39630	0.11290	3.51	0.000
	Members aware of objectives	−0.13904	0.13834	−1.01	0.315
	Members aware of rules	−0.02117	0.13010	−0.16	0.871
	Representatives aware of rules	0.17093	0.08241	2.07	0.038
	Meeting minutes read	0.06344	0.09556	0.66	0.507
	Meeting minutes orally informed	0.49163	0.13806	3.56	0.000
	Meeting minutes available upon request	0.04071	0.09592	0.42	0.671
	Linkages with gram panchayats (KA)	−0.86315	0.26241	−3.29	0.001
	Linkages with gram panchayats (UA)	−0.35536	0.15382	−2.31	0.021
	Linkages with other local organizations (KA)	−0.54159	0.16295	−3.32	0.001
	Linkages with other local organizations (UA)	−0.05561	0.13954	−0.40	0.690
	Linkages with line department (KA)	−0.30808	0.19856	−1.55	0.121
	Linkages with line department (UA)	0.38505	0.11847	3.25	0.001
	Caste: scheduled tribe	−0.27478	0.17086	−1.61	0.108
	Caste: backward caste	0.11230	0.18240	0.62	0.538
	Caste: forward caste	0.45652	0.13507	3.38	0.001
	Caste: minority	0.78544	0.22493	3.49	0.000
	Poverty ranking: poor	−0.05805	0.09569	−0.61	0.544
	Poverty ranking: middle	0.12459	0.09557	1.30	0.192
	Poverty ranking: wealthy	0.00982	0.10505	0.09	0.926
	Landholding: 0–1 acre	0.06568	0.17301	0.38	0.704
	Landholding: 1–2.5 acres	0.16969	0.17291	0.98	0.326
	Landholding: 2.5–5 acres	0.03746	0.15961	0.23	0.814
	Landholding: 5–10 acres	0.08952	0.16391	0.55	0.585

(Table continues on the following pages.)

Table A32 (*continued*)

Function	Variable	Coefficient	Robust standard error	z-value	p-value
	Landholding: 10+ acres	0.14840	0.16565	0.90	0.370
	Woman-headed household	0.17696	0.10165	1.74	0.082
	Distance to market	0.13151	0.06411	2.05	0.040
	Irrigated land	0.02250	0.01874	1.20	0.230
	Number of households	0.33477	0.07212	4.64	0.000
	Uttaranchal	−0.70655	0.39203	−1.80	0.072
	CBO-GI	−0.50191	0.13245	−3.79	0.000
	Subfunction #6 dummy	−0.93887	0.15476	−6.07	0.000
	Subfunction #9 dummy	−0.18503	0.16640	−1.11	0.266
	Subfunction #10 dummy	−0.84642	0.23468	−3.61	0.000
	Subfunction #11 dummy	−0.21578	0.07646	−2.82	0.005
	Constant: lower boundary	0.93711	0.58603	1.60	0.110
	Constant: upper boundary	2.44804	0.58384	4.19	0.000
Community-based action (N = 454)					
	Human assets	−1.66554	0.54231	−3.07	0.002
	Material assets	2.54296	0.72756	3.50	0.000
	Financial assets	0.16144	0.18157	0.89	0.374
	Households attend meetings	0.24829	0.17975	1.38	0.167
	Always conducts self-monitoring	0.76400	0.25969	2.94	0.003
	Members aware of objectives	2.26426	0.45215	5.01	0.000
	Members aware of rules	−1.15665	0.34874	−3.32	0.001
	Representatives aware of rules	0.57310	0.31779	1.80	0.071
	Meeting minutes read	0.19736	0.21210	0.93	0.352
	Meeting minutes orally informed	0.59401	0.33116	1.79	0.073
	Meeting minutes available upon request	−0.57753	0.26093	−2.21	0.027
	Linkages with gram panchayats (UA)	−0.12212	0.42865	−0.28	0.776
	Linkages with other local organizations (KA)	0.50584	1.34378	0.38	0.707
	Linkages with other local organizations (UA)	−0.82368	0.30480	−2.70	0.007

Table A32 (*continued*)

Function	Variable	Coefficient	Robust standard error	z-value	p-value
	Linkages with line department (KA)	−0.40516	1.35849	−0.30	0.766
	Linkages with line department (UA)	2.14151	0.26123	8.20	0.000
	Caste: scheduled tribe	0.82016	0.58268	1.41	0.159
	Caste: backward caste	1.09109	0.51664	2.11	0.035
	Caste: forward caste	0.34600	0.22819	1.52	0.129
	Caste: minority	0.74816	0.56120	1.33	0.182
	Poverty ranking: poor	−0.10322	0.18756	−0.55	0.582
	Poverty ranking: middle	0.19787	0.19596	1.01	0.313
	Poverty ranking: wealthy	0.22454	0.21331	1.05	0.293
	Landholding: 0–1 acre	−0.40581	0.28458	−1.43	0.154
	Landholding: 1–2.5 acres	−0.33078	0.29934	−1.11	0.269
	Landholding: 2.5–5 acres	−0.19979	0.28325	−0.71	0.481
	Landholding: 5–10 acres	−0.14283	0.29895	−0.48	0.633
	Landholding: 10+ acres	−0.45075	0.35042	−1.29	0.198
	Woman-headed household	0.18433	0.19194	0.96	0.337
	Distance to market	0.94787	0.19763	4.80	0.000
	Irrigated land	−0.12440	0.06825	−1.82	0.068
	Number of households	−0.71799	0.20961	−3.43	0.001
	Uttaranchal	3.00853	0.96176	3.13	0.002
	CBO-GI	−0.70331	0.64715	−1.09	0.277
	Subfunction #13 dummy	−0.13311	0.12134	−1.10	0.273
	Constant: lower boundary	0.63426	1.45923	0.43	0.664
	Constant: upper boundary	3.64759	1.48091	2.46	0.014
Capacity building (N = 1,931)					
	Human assets	−0.38662	0.11250	−3.44	0.001
	Material assets	−0.38922	0.11739	−3.32	0.001
	Financial assets	1.06805	0.11648	9.17	0.000
	Households attend meetings	0.00889	0.09018	0.10	0.921
	Always conducts self-monitoring	1.17129	0.12208	9.59	0.000
	Members aware of objectives	−0.12157	0.15136	−0.80	0.422
	Members aware of rules	0.05643	0.14672	0.38	0.701

(Table continues on the following pages.)

Table A32 (*continued*)

Function	Variable	Coefficient	Robust standard error	z-value	p-value
	Representatives aware of rules	−0.05484	0.09819	−0.56	0.576
	Meeting minutes read	−0.07819	0.10081	−0.78	0.438
	Meeting minutes orally informed	0.57955	0.14813	3.91	0.000
	Meeting minutes available upon request	−0.39131	0.10752	−3.64	0.000
	Linkages with gram panchayats (KA)	−0.65592	0.18504	−3.54	0.000
	Linkages with gram panchayats (UA)	−0.42284	0.16381	−2.58	0.010
	Linkages with other local organizations (KA)	−0.03272	0.13382	−0.24	0.807
	Linkages with other local organizations (UA)	−1.02875	0.16188	−6.35	0.000
	Linkages with line department (KA)	0.76564	0.19229	3.98	0.000
	Linkages with line department (UA)	0.81548	0.15851	5.14	0.000
	Caste: scheduled tribe	−0.14985	0.16201	−0.92	0.355
	Caste: backward caste	−0.05238	0.15250	−0.34	0.731
	Caste: forward caste	0.05231	0.12487	0.42	0.675
	Caste: minority	0.93250	0.22395	4.16	0.000
	Poverty ranking: poor	0.06208	0.11714	0.53	0.596
	Poverty ranking: middle	0.17730	0.10935	1.62	0.105
	Poverty ranking: wealthy	0.22466	0.12627	1.78	0.075
	Landholding: 0–1 acre	0.11321	0.19773	0.57	0.567
	Landholding: 1–2.5 acres	0.25649	0.20203	1.27	0.204
	Landholding: 2.5–5 acres	0.20292	0.18197	1.12	0.265
	Landholding: 5–10 acres	0.32349	0.18585	1.74	0.082
	Landholding: 10+ acres	0.14972	0.18330	0.82	0.414
	Woman-headed household	−0.02118	0.11407	−0.19	0.853
	Distance to market	0.42901	0.06553	6.55	0.000
	Irrigated land	−0.05984	0.01954	−3.06	0.002
	Number of households	0.33797	0.08936	3.78	0.000
	Uttaranchal	0.68233	0.35919	1.90	0.057

Table A32 (*continued*)

Function	Variable	Coefficient	Robust standard error	z-value	p-value
	CBO-GI	−0.25313	0.15656	−1.62	0.106
	Subfunction #16 dummy	0.82788	0.06596	12.55	0.000
	Subfunction #17 dummy	0.91922	0.06987	13.16	0.000
	Constant: lower boundary	3.34596	0.63108	5.30	0.000
	Constant: upper boundary	4.98047	0.64502	7.72	0.000
Coordination of activities (N = 664)					
	Human assets	−0.82017	0.20403	−4.02	0.000
	Material assets	−0.46512	0.15866	−2.93	0.003
	Financial assets	0.93694	0.13878	6.75	0.000
	Households attend meetings	−0.09684	0.12583	−0.77	0.442
	Always conducts self-monitoring	0.09030	0.17535	0.51	0.607
	Members aware of objectives	−0.37593	0.18889	−1.99	0.047
	Members aware of rules	0.58917	0.20012	2.94	0.003
	Representatives aware of rules	0.40045	0.12869	3.11	0.002
	Meeting minutes read	−0.03531	0.11782	−0.30	0.764
	Meeting minutes orally informed	0.34898	0.16227	2.15	0.032
	Meeting minutes available upon request	−0.29681	0.15724	−1.89	0.059
	Linkages with gram panchayats (KA)	−0.71972	0.36395	−1.98	0.048
	Linkages with gram panchayats (UA)	−0.68863	0.22522	−3.06	0.002
	Linkages with other local organizations (KA)	0.53825	0.23247	2.32	0.021
	Linkages with other local organizations (UA)	−0.48510	0.20004	−2.43	0.015
	Linkages with line department (KA)	−0.21995	0.31256	−0.70	0.482
	Linkages with line department (UA)	0.67193	0.16104	4.17	0.000
	Caste: scheduled tribe	0.44029	0.23967	1.84	0.066
	Caste: backward caste	0.63681	0.25311	2.52	0.012
	Caste: forward caste	0.45843	0.16676	2.75	0.006

(Table continues on the following pages.)

Table A32 (continued)

Function	Variable	Coefficient	Robust standard error	z-value	p-value
	Caste: minority	1.41285	0.31084	4.55	0.000
	Poverty ranking: poor	0.11069	0.15097	0.73	0.463
	Poverty ranking: middle	0.21551	0.13049	1.65	0.099
	Poverty ranking: wealthy	0.22621	0.15177	1.49	0.136
	Landholding: 0–1 acre	0.25724	0.24003	1.07	0.284
	Landholding: 1–2.5 acres	0.00802	0.27244	0.03	0.977
	Landholding: 2.5–5 acres	0.30086	0.25487	1.18	0.238
	Landholding: 5–10 acres	−0.03677	0.25134	−0.15	0.884
	Landholding: 10+ acres	−0.02027	0.25405	−0.08	0.936
	Woman-headed household	−0.02908	0.14022	−0.21	0.836
	Distance to market	0.63892	0.08853	7.22	0.000
	Irrigated land	0.12381	0.03199	3.87	0.000
	Number of households	0.15447	0.13658	1.13	0.258
	Uttaranchal	2.17152	0.49538	4.38	0.000
	CBO-GI	1.07657	0.20235	5.32	0.000
	Subfunction #18 dummy	−0.67245	0.14348	−4.69	0.000
	Subfunction #19 dummy	−0.07906	0.12174	−0.65	0.516
	Constant: lower boundary	3.22976	0.90582	3.57	0.000
	Constant: upper boundary	5.02269	0.91275	5.50	0.000
Monitoring and evaluation (N = 741)					
	Human assets	−0.67824	0.15207	−4.46	0.000
	Material assets	−0.38161	0.15222	−2.51	0.012
	Financial assets	1.20563	0.15707	7.68	0.000
	Households attend meetings	−0.11008	0.11623	−0.95	0.344
	Always conducts self-monitoring	0.52986	0.17285	3.07	0.002
	Members aware of objectives	0.05749	0.17311	0.33	0.740
	Members aware of rules	−0.37631	0.20761	−1.81	0.070
	Representatives aware of rules	−0.14069	0.11277	−1.25	0.212
	Meeting minutes read	0.22833	0.13249	1.72	0.085
	Meeting minutes orally informed	0.35059	0.20434	1.72	0.086
	Meeting minutes available upon request	−0.21638	0.12763	−1.70	0.090

Table A32 (*continued*)

Function	Variable	Coefficient	Robust standard error	z-value	p-value
	Linkages with gram panchayats (KA)	−0.20871	0.32673	−0.64	0.523
	Linkages with gram panchayats (UA)	0.36453	0.21481	1.70	0.090
	Linkages with other local organizations (KA)	−0.04136	0.20769	−0.20	0.842
	Linkages with other local organizations (UA)	−1.49668	0.23591	−6.34	0.000
	Linkages with line department (KA)	0.45377	0.27570	1.65	0.100
	Linkages with line department (UA)	0.72565	0.19826	3.66	0.000
	Caste: scheduled tribe	0.38673	0.22479	1.72	0.085
	Caste: backward caste	0.12135	0.22194	0.55	0.585
	Caste: forward caste	0.23607	0.16843	1.40	0.161
	Caste: minority	1.10862	0.29038	3.82	0.000
	Poverty ranking: poor	0.03848	0.15757	0.24	0.807
	Poverty ranking: middle	0.00256	0.14697	0.02	0.986
	Poverty ranking: wealthy	0.11447	0.15630	0.73	0.464
	Landholding: 0–1 acre	0.45166	0.21853	2.07	0.039
	Landholding: 1–2.5 acres	0.27321	0.22348	1.22	0.222
	Landholding: 2.5–5 acres	0.30581	0.21907	1.40	0.163
	Landholding: 5–10 acres	0.27359	0.23230	1.18	0.239
	Landholding: 10+ acres	0.31370	0.23391	1.34	0.180
	Woman-headed household	0.01026	0.14879	0.07	0.945
	Distance to market	0.36319	0.08656	4.20	0.000
	Irrigated land	0.03733	0.02755	1.35	0.175
	Number of households	0.51033	0.13428	3.80	0.000
	Uttaranchal	0.77264	0.47250	1.64	0.102
	CBO-GI	−0.99916	0.18374	−5.44	0.000
	Constant: lower boundary	2.45021	0.87846	2.79	0.005
	Constant: upper boundary	4.56176	0.89222	5.11	0.000
Conflict resolution and accountability (N = 1,162)					
	Human assets	−0.37585	0.11377	−3.30	0.001
	Material assets	−0.24448	0.10980	−2.23	0.026

(*Table continues on the following pages.*)

Table A32 (*continued*)

Function	Variable	Coefficient	Robust standard error	z-value	p-value
	Financial assets	1.26928	0.12181	10.42	0.000
	Households attend meetings	−0.05842	0.08456	−0.69	0.490
	Always conducts self-monitoring	1.14068	0.13956	8.17	0.000
	Members aware of objectives	−0.92391	0.15376	−6.01	0.000
	Members aware of rules	−0.35331	0.15409	−2.29	0.022
	Representatives aware of rules	0.03690	0.09500	0.39	0.698
	Meeting minutes read	−0.09632	0.10070	−0.96	0.339
	Meeting minutes orally informed	0.41642	0.15002	2.78	0.006
	Meeting minutes available upon request	−0.08220	0.10953	−0.75	0.453
	Linkages with gram panchayats (KA)	−0.13305	0.18677	−0.71	0.476
	Linkages with gram panchayats (UA)	0.53037	0.18383	2.89	0.004
	Linkages with other local organizations (KA)	−0.21224	0.13617	−1.56	0.119
	Linkages with other local organizations (UA)	−0.47290	0.19627	−2.41	0.016
	Linkages with line department (KA)	−0.18290	0.17546	−1.04	0.297
	Linkages with line department (UA)	0.65181	0.15962	4.08	0.000
	Caste: scheduled tribe	0.34844	0.14093	2.47	0.013
	Caste: backward caste	0.38706	0.15210	2.54	0.011
	Caste: forward caste	0.42673	0.11714	3.64	0.000
	Caste: minority	0.89148	0.30843	2.89	0.004
	Poverty ranking: poor	0.11733	0.11255	1.04	0.297
	Poverty ranking: middle	0.08025	0.11019	0.73	0.466
	Poverty ranking: wealthy	0.07964	0.12601	0.63	0.527
	Landholding: 0–1 acre	−0.56606	0.19506	−2.90	0.004
	Landholding: 1–2.5 acres	−0.19027	0.20196	−0.94	0.346
	Landholding: 2.5–5 acres	0.21331	0.18722	1.14	0.255
	Landholding: 5–10 acres	0.18051	0.18728	0.96	0.335
	Landholding: 10+ acres	0.04383	0.17887	0.25	0.806

Table A32 (continued)

Function	Variable	Coefficient	Robust standard error	z-value	p-value
	Woman-headed household	−0.06546	0.11746	−0.56	0.577
	Distance to market	0.07536	0.06453	1.17	0.243
	Irrigated land	0.00863	0.01969	0.44	0.661
	Number of households	0.64101	0.08821	7.27	0.000
	Uttaranchal	1.38194	0.34967	3.95	0.000
	CBO-GI	−0.87446	0.13501	−6.48	0.000
	Subfunction #22 dummy	−0.66770	0.12341	−5.41	0.000
	Subfunction #23 dummy	−1.33745	0.10760	−12.43	0.000
	Constant: lower boundary	2.50161	0.60654	4.12	0.000
	Constant: upper boundary	4.05436	0.61164	6.63	0.000
Information sharing and dissemination (N = 515)					
	Human assets	−0.24885	0.20128	−1.24	0.216
	Material assets	−0.67804	0.19625	−3.45	0.001
	Financial assets	1.29035	0.18408	7.01	0.000
	Households attend meetings	0.34065	0.14323	2.38	0.017
	Always conducts self-monitoring	0.93085	0.20894	4.46	0.000
	Members aware of objectives	0.18161	0.22909	0.79	0.428
	Members aware of rules	−0.71368	0.24713	−2.89	0.004
	Representatives aware of rules	0.72671	0.15930	4.56	0.000
	Meeting minutes read	0.19948	0.17777	1.12	0.262
	Meeting minutes orally informed	0.24109	0.25893	0.93	0.352
	Meeting minutes available upon request	−0.10854	0.19423	−0.56	0.576
	Linkages with gram panchayats (KA)	−0.92248	0.33016	−2.79	0.005
	Linkages with gram panchayats (UA)	−1.12885	0.29252	−3.86	0.000
	Linkages with other local organizations (KA)	−0.56761	0.25763	−2.20	0.028
	Linkages with other local organizations (UA)	0.16040	0.28617	0.56	0.575
	Linkages with line department (KA)	0.67436	0.33051	2.04	0.041

(Table continues on the following pages.)

Table A32 (concluded)

Function	Variable	Coefficient	Robust standard error	z-value	p-value
	Linkages with line department (UA)	0.28903	0.21023	1.37	0.169
	Caste: scheduled tribe	−0.34452	0.28955	−1.19	0.234
	Caste: backward caste	−0.26820	0.29597	−0.91	0.365
	Caste: forward caste	0.21983	0.21797	1.01	0.313
	Caste: minority	−0.35515	0.48386	−0.73	0.463
	Poverty ranking: poor	−0.14112	0.17840	−0.79	0.429
	Poverty ranking: middle	−0.21068	0.17122	−1.23	0.219
	Poverty ranking: wealthy	−0.09503	0.19592	−0.49	0.628
	Landholding: 0–1 acre	−0.59299	0.39155	−1.51	0.130
	Landholding: 1–2.5 acres	−0.42044	0.41462	−1.01	0.311
	Landholding: 2.5–5 acres	−0.21206	0.40370	−0.53	0.599
	Landholding: 5–10 acres	−0.08008	0.40529	−0.20	0.843
	Landholding: 10+ acres	−0.25278	0.40023	−0.63	0.528
	Woman-headed household	−0.39589	0.16455	−2.41	0.016
	Distance to market	0.62479	0.11064	5.65	0.000
	Irrigated land	0.04303	0.05978	0.72	0.472
	Number of households	0.46997	0.12159	3.87	0.000
	Uttaranchal	2.70109	0.59029	4.58	0.000
	CBO-GI	−1.11496	0.24136	−4.62	0.000
	Constant: lower boundary	3.45804	1.06337	3.25	0.001
	Constant: upper boundary	5.37734	1.08219	4.97	0.000

Sources: Household questionnaire, local organization officials questionnaire, and GP elected functionaries questionnaire.

Note: CBO-GI = community-based organization (government-initiated); CBO-NI = community-based organization (NGO-initiated); KA = Karnataka; MP = Madhya Pradesh; UA = Uttaranchal.

Index